WITHDRAWN

PATHWAYS TO ELFLAND: The Writings of Lord Dunsany

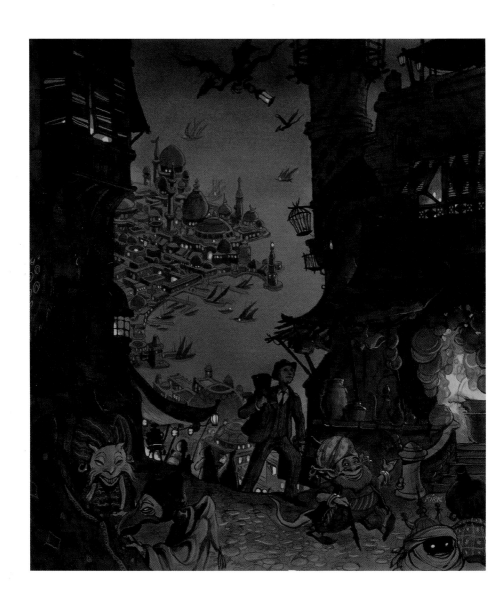

PATHWAYS TO ELFLAND: The Writings of Lord Dunsany

by Darrell Schweitzer

Foreword by
L. Sprague de Camp

Illustrations by
Tim Kirk

Öwlswick Press   Philadelphia

Portions of this book have been previously published in different form:
  "The Novels of Lord Dunsany," in *Mythlore*, numbers 25 & 26, copyright © 1980 & 1981 by The Mythopoeic Society.
  "Lord Dunsany: The Plays," in *Nyctalops*, number 16, copyright © 1981 by Harry O. Morris, Jr.

[iv]

Contents

Foreword by L. Sprague de Camp vii
Acknowledgements xiv

Introduction 1
Early Short Stories 6
Plays 40
Novels 76
Later Short Stories 110
Poetry 127
Non-Fiction 137
Uncollected Works 146
Conclusion 155

Appendix 158
Bibliography 163
Index 173

Illustrations

" 'Why! you will beat me yet.' "
   from "A Losing Game" 35
" 'There's plenty of hope there, isn't there?' "
   from *The Glittering Gate* 57
"Such speed was new to the dog."
   from *The King of Elfland's Daughter* 89

Foreword

I first met Lord Dunsany's work in the 1920s when, as a high-school student, I stumbled upon *The Book of Wonder* in a public library in Hollywood, California. Like many young readers, I was "struck all of a heap" by the charm of Dunsany's style and the grandeur of his imagination. Over the years I picked up copies of his other books until I had built up a fair collection of them. In 1952, when Willy Ley and I published *Lands Beyond*, I sent a copy to Lord Dunsany with a fan letter and received a pleasant reply. In 1958, my wife and I were planning a trip to Britain and France, and I meant to take my courage in my hands and ask Dunsany for permission to call—only to read of his death.

A few years later, I learned that Lady Dunsany was selling off surplus copies of the author's books, which had been stacked in the attic of Dunstall Priory, the Dunsanys' house in Kent, and I bought several copies to round out my collection. Thus began a correspondence, which continued until Lady Dunsany's death a decade ago. In 1963 I began editing a series of anthologies of heroic fantasy, each time using a Dunsany story. That summer, when Catherine and I made an automobile trip through England and Wales, we visited Lady Dunsany in Kent.

Dunstall Priory—so named because there was once a real priory on the site—proved a rambling two-story Regency house, set on rolling meadows well back from the country road. A stand in the vestibule held several of Dunsany's walking sticks, while three cloaks and several of his campaign hats (the stiff-brimmed kind that WWI American soldiers and Boy Scouts used to wear) hung on pegs along the wall.

The living room and library had a bay window in which Dunsany's desk still stood. The room was papered with scenic French wallpaper. When Catherine wondered how they had found wallpaper so right for the period of the house, Lady Dunsany said: "But my dear, this is the original!" Every twenty years or so, for a century and a half, craftsmen had soaked off the old paper, cleaned it, mended it, and put it back in place.

The upper bookshelves held long lines of bound manuscript volumes, entirely written in Dunsany's scribbly but fairly legible longhand. Catherine asked Lady Dunsany if she was familiar with a fragment by Lord Dunsany beginning: "What is it to hate poetry?" Lady Dunsany said: "Oh, do you know that passage, my dear?"

"Yes," said Catherine. "I used to read it to my students when I was an English teacher, but I never found out when he wrote it."

Lady Dunsany murmured: "Let me see—that was in a speech delivered in Scotland in 1902 at a medical convocation." Her thin old hand pulled a volume off the shelf, handed it to Catherine, and she said: "Will you read it to me, my dear?"

So Catherine, much thrilled, read: " . . . for what is it to hate poetry? It is to have no little dreams and fancies, no holy memories of golden days, to be unmoved by serene midsummer evenings or dawn over wild lands, singing or sunshine, little tales told by the fire a long while since, glow-worms and briar-rose; for of all these things and more is poetry made. It is to be cut off for ever from the fellowship of great men that are gone; to see men and women without their haloes and the world without its glory; to miss the meaning lurking behind common things, like elves hiding in flowers; it is to beat one's hands all day against the gates of Fairyland, and to find that they are shut and the country empty and its kings gone hence."*

Beatrice Villiers Plunkett, Dowager Lady Dunsany, was a slender woman in her eighties, a little above average height and young-looking for her age. A water-color portrait on the wall showed that she had been quite a beautiful young woman. Although she appeared active and in good health, she said: "But I'm so *old*, you know." She seemed to be living largely in the past, with little interest in "obscene" modern literature.

Catherine asked her to describe Dunsany at his work. So she showed how he sat at right angles to the bay windows, quill pen in hand, scribbling in a leather-bound notebook the one and only draft of his writings. In answer to a tactful question, she confirmed my suspicion that he was a temperamental and often difficult man. But she evidently

---

*Dunsany: *Nowadays* (1918), pp. 21f.

[ix]

still idealized him, somewhat as the widow of Dunsany's relative, the even more difficult Captain Sir Richard Francis Burton, idealized Burton.

We had lunch on priceless 18th-century Chinese export china—a few meager sardines and a fresh salad—but the thimbleful of sherry was excellent, as were the fine old silver and china on the antique table. Lady Dunsany told us how, when they were living at Castle Dunsany in Ireland during the Troubles, their gardener confided that he had learned he would be murdered by the IRA unless he could borrow ten pounds to flee to Canada. Dunsany lent the money and forgot the matter. One night years later, after Dunsany had given a lecture in Chicago, a ruddy, prosperous-looking, middle-aged man came up saying: "Here's the ten pounds I owe you."

We visited the Roman excavations at nearby Lullingstone Manor with Lady Dunsany and then took our leave, promising more checks for the use of Dunsany's stories. "They will be very welcome," said Lady Dunsany, showing that for all the fine furnishings she was none too well off.

In 1967, when Alan Nourse and I stopped in London on our way back from India, I again went to Dunstall Priory by train and taxi. Lady Dunsany showed me an album of pictures of Castle Dunsany, where the Dunsanys' son Randal Plunkett, now the nineteenth baron, lives. The castle goes back several centuries, but was drastically modernized about two centuries ago. Surrounded by gravel paths instead of a moat, it now looks more like a big country house set amid gardens. She said: "If you're going to modernize a castle, the eighteenth century is the very best time to do it."

[x]

FOREWORD

We continued our correspondence until Lady Dunsany died. When Catherine and I took our grandson to Ireland in 1971, we reminded the present Lord Dunsany of his invitation to visit the place. At the entrance I saw what looked like a half-ruined square Norman guard tower and later asked Lord Dunsany about it.

"Oh, that's just a folly," he replied. The structure was one of those synthetic medieval ruins that landowners put up in the early nineteenth century to express the spirit of the Romantic Era. The interior of the castle had an overlay of 18th-century Adam architecture, with a wide marble stair going up from the entrance hall. On the walls were Sidney Sime's original drawings for Dunsany's stories. Dunsany (the eighteenth, that is) had done some weird drawings—talented amateur work, comparable to that of Clark Ashton Smith.

The two-story drawing room was lined with bookcases, and when the present Dunsany pressed a place on the wall, a bookcase swung open to reveal a stair going down to a hidden room. This was the "priest hole"—a hiding place for Catholic priests during the periods of persecution in the seventeenth century, before the Dunsanys converted to Protestantism. One relative, Oliver Plunkett, Archbishop of Dublin, was one of Titus Oates's last victims, being framed on charges of plotting a French invasion and being hanged, drawn, and quartered. He is now a saint.

Catherine poured tea, while our grandson and I carried on a lively conversation with the present Lord Dunsany about his part in the battle of El Alamein, in which he commanded an armored-car unit of the Guides Cavalry of the Indian Army. At one point he said: "Back in the days of Empire, the Irish made excellent colonial civil servants. Having grown up in an atmosphere of hospitality, flattery, treachery, and murder, they weren't surprised when they encountered these things in the colonies."

Darrell Schweitzer's book is timely and, in fact, overdue. A number of pieces have been written about the eighteenth Dunsany, such as Dr. Oliver St. John Gogarty's memoir in the *Atlantic Monthly* for March 1955, and Mark Amory's book-length biography. But nobody has done a book-length study of all the writings of the most influential fantasy writer of this century. E. H. Bierstadt's *Dunsany the Dramatist* (1917) dealt only with the early plays.

Now we have a thoughtful study of the whole great corpus. I find only a few minor points of disagreement with Darrell. While I support his generally negative opinion of Dunsany's poetry, I think Dunsany made at least one good poem, *The Last Wolf*:

> The last wolf in England
> Was lean and very old,
> The last wolf in England
> Was shivering with the cold. . . .

But appreciation of poetry is highly subjective at best. And, while *The Last Revolution* does, as Darrell says, have an old-fashioned science-fiction story quality, it is still highly readable and a striking example of the skillful build-up of tension.

But you should judge Darrell's arguments for yourself. Few have read more than a fraction of Dunsany's output,

FOREWORD

and these pages may lead you to a literary feast that may
well delight you.

L. Sprague de Camp
Villanova, Pennsylvania
February 1979

Acknowledgements

The author would like to thank L. Sprague de Camp, Dirk Mosig, Mark Owings, and Mark Mansell for help in obtaining materials for this project. Apologies are due to anyone I have forgotten. Thanks are also in order to Donald G. Keller for encouraging me to get on with this work more years ago than I care to remember.

Darrell Schweitzer

PATHWAYS

TO

ELFLAND

[xvi]

Introduction

The marvelous work of Edward John More-
ton Drax Plunkett, the 18th Baron Dunsany (1878–1957)
is not as well known as it should be, and this book is an
attempt to rectify the situation. Most fantasy readers today
know his name, but have little idea of the extent of his
total output, what kind of writing it is, or how good it is.
That is what I propose to tell you.

Dunsany is known today primarily through the efforts
of Lin Carter, who published (incredible as it seems) the
first paperbacks of Dunsany ever, as part of the Ballantine
Adult Fantasy Series in the early 1970s. Dunsany had flour-
ished and even enjoyed considerable critical reputation in
the early part of this century, but went into eclipse during
that period, roughly the Depression through the early '60s,
when critics and English Literature professors were insisting that realism was somehow a more "serious" and
loftier type of art than fantasy could ever be. In the long
view of literature, this dogma is extremely provincial, considering that fantasy has been with us from the very first,
in the ancient epics, in the Latin and Greek novels which

[1]

were popular in later classical times (*The Golden Ass* of Lucius Apuleius, the *Aethiopica* of Heliodorus, etc.), in the medieval romances, *The Arabian Nights*, Jonathan Swift, the satirical romances of Voltaire, the Gothic novel, the Victorian ghost story, Mark Twain's *Connecticut Yankee* and *Mysterious Stranger*, and so on. One is tempted to say that the fashion for realism of the Hemingway-Faulkner-Fitzgerald variety is a temporary aberration, and the current resurgence of the fantastic is merely the taste of the reading public reverting to normal. But it is more complicated than that. Dunsany's delicate fancies will never appeal to a genuinely mass audience any more than the metaphysical fables of Jorge Luis Borges will, because it takes a special sort of imagination to appreciate them, and particularly in such cases, books which are out of print tend to stay that way. Connoisseurs know about them, and they may bring high prices second hand, but when an editor goes into a commercial publisher's office and says, "Let's do Dunsany," the publisher will pull *Books In Print* down off the shelf and say, "Nobody else is doing Dunsany. It must not be profitable." So when Lin Carter managed to get some Dunsany into mass-market paperbacks, he really started something, and he deserves the credit. Suddenly a new generation of readers discovered splendid, timeless fantasies which remain as fresh as they were when first published, some of them as many as seventy years ago.

The present volume is not a biography. Mark Amory's *Lord Dunsany: A Biography* (Collins, 1972) is excellent, and since I cannot improve on it, it would be senseless to repeat what he has done. All references to Amory are to the biography. The other principal sources for information on

INTRODUCTION

Dunsany are the three volumes of autobiography, *Patches of Sunlight*, *While The Sirens Slept*, and *The Sirens Wake*, which cover those parts of Dunsany's life he cared to make public, up through World War II.

For the benefit of those who have read none of these, herewith a brief sketch:

Dunsany's early life very much resembles that of the young Winston Churchill, save that he gave up on politics after losing his first election, and went into literature. He was born in England to a very old line of Anglo-Irish nobility, educated at Eton and Sandhurst, after which he joined the Coldstream Guards, went off to Gibraltar, and then to Africa, where he saw action in the Boer War. Afterwards he spent half his time in England, half in Ireland, where the family owned an estate and castle in County Meath. He ran for Parliament, lost by fourteen hundred votes, withdrew from public life, and like many young aristocrats of the day, settled down to wasting his time splendidly with a wide variety of idle amusements, mostly hunting. Dunsany was a lifelong sportsman, and his autobiographies are filled with casual mentions of incredible totals of slaughtered wildlife which tend to appall the modern reader. One gets the impression he alone was responsible for putting half the creatures on the Endangered Species list at the brink of oblivion.

In his early twenties, even after he had married Beatrice, the daughter of the Earl of Jersey, he still had no idea what he wanted to do with his life. He was a classic specimen of what George Bernard Shaw called the "Idle Rich Class." He was addicted to parlor games and schoolboy antics; having Beatrice drop balloons from a balcony so he could shoot them with a toy gun, sailing model ships loaded with firecrackers into the middle of a pond to blow up and sink in a satisfying manner; not to mention rounds of partying, some travel, and chess, at which he became champion of Ireland at one point. Being independently wealthy, he never needed anything approximating a job.

Chances are, anyone who knew him about 1903 would never have guess he was destined to become an author, but he was in a perfect position to do so. He had had interesting experiences. He was well-read and educated. He was financially secure to the point that he had no need to make a living off his work at first, and thus could experiment with anything he wanted instead of rushing to produce what sold best. Also, he seems to have had an overwhelming talent from the very beginning. He wrote very little in his youth, and did not leave behind a long series of amateur botches and juvenilia. He served virtually no apprenticeship. Before his career proper began, he had composed a few poems, sold one to *The Pall Mall Magazine* at the age of sixteen, and while at Sandhurst made his first attempt at a short story, in collaboration with Lord Howard de Walden, who was in the same company. He describes the effort in *Patches of Sunlight*:

> . . . and [he] suggested that we should write a tale together about how the Great Thirst came to R.M.C. [Royal Military College], being caught from a missionary who had been preaching in the Sahara, and how it spread like an epidemic as far as Aldershot. So I wrote some of it, and Lord Howard de Walden wrote

[4]

some; and then the novelty of authorship wore off, and we never finished the tale.

(p.78)

Then suddenly, in 1904, *The Gods of Pegāna* burst into existence. Dunsany was a natural from the start, with tremendous powers of organization. He simply sat down and wrote, never revising, because when he wrote, revising was never necessary. This is to say that he probably composed his tales unconsciously in his head, letting them grow slowly out of images, scenes, remembered lines of poetry, or whatever, until everything flowed forth in already finished form. Sometimes he wrote with a quill pen; sometimes he dictated to Beatrice.

It was with *The Gods of Pegāna* that his career and reputation began.

[5]

Early Short Stories

Influences Dunsany acknowledged included Herodotus, the King James Bible, Grimms' and Andersen's fairy tales, and the proceedings of the divorce courts; the latter because their presence caused his mother to forbid him to read newspapers as a child, forcing him on to the former. Also, his studies of Greek and Latin no doubt gave him a greater mastery over his own tongue. Some of the patterns of Irish daily speech are blended into his style, giving it a unique flavor. He had a good ear for language from the start, a natural eloquence which helped when he was delivering lectures, and which doubtless made the dictating of tales easy for him.

Prose, to him, was a matter of rhythm:

> . . . rhythm is a matter of sound, and prose that does not sound well when properly read, and aloud, is not in my opinion good prose . . .

And though the sound of words may be dismissed by some as only a matter of opinion, incapable of proof, that is not so when they are spoken to an audience; and the response to words that are rightly strung together is immediate . . .

Prose then learns its rhythm from speech, and rhythm is a kind of chariot that rattles through into the attention of man; past prejudices, distractions, and all manner of obstacles, right into the inner citadel of his consciousness: and why this is so I cannot say, but the fact remains that if a man starts his story with such words as

In Padan Aram in the field of Luz,

the ears of the world will be turned to him; while words of profoundest import, plodding their way barefooted without that chariot called Rhythm, scarce come within sight of the ardours that dwell in the reason of man.

(Patches of Sunlight, pp. 132)

Actual precedents for the type of story he began to write are harder to find. One might point to the early stories of William Butler Yeats and the fairy tales of Oscar Wilde. He was strongly stimulated to write by *The Darling of the Gods*, a play he saw in 1904, which impressed him with its marvelous and largely imaginary version of Japan because it pointed out the direction in which he wanted to go; but he practically invented a new form as he went along.

Adhering to his own principles on the construction of prose, he began thus:

Before there stood gods upon Olympus, or ever

[7]

PATHWAYS TO ELFLAND

> Allah was Allah, had wrought and rested **Mana-Yood-Sushai**.
> There are in Pegāna—Mung and Sish and Kib, and the maker of all small gods, who is **Mana-Yood-Sushai**. Moreover we have faith in Roon and Slid.
>
> (p. 1)

The volume is a collection of inter-connected short pieces, and there is nothing quite like them in all of literature. A mixture of myth, fable, and occasional mirth, the whole resembles a scripture of an unknown religion. It even contains litanies to the gods.

Such a book from an unknown writer is hardly a commercial prospect, so Dunsany's wealth did posterity a service. When Elkin Matthews brought the volume out in the autumn of 1905, the author paid the cost of printing. It drew a sufficiently favorable response to insure more professional publication in the future. *The Gods of Pegāna* was Dunsany's only "vanity" press item, and that only in its first edition.

Stylistically, the work is thickly archaic, graceful, and reminiscent of the King James Bible. In subject matter, it is a triumph of the imagination. It exists sheerly for exoticism and beauty. Surely there is no religious significance, and those looking for allegorical meanings are bound to be disappointed. Dunsany was an atheist, and also a believer in art for art's sake.

This first effort showed staggering powers of invention, and also an ability to handle the numinous. Dunsany had the good sense to approach things beyond human ken indirectly, to hint and imply rather than display his deities

[8]

like butterflies pinned in a collection. Always Pegāna and her inhabitants remain half seen in the distance, and we are led to suspect that what has been revealed to us about them has been filtered and simplified by human minds. The worldview is primitive, which serves to make the gods plausible. Animism and the personification of natural forces, two mainstays of ancient beliefs, abound: and thus it only seems fitting that Night and Morning should meet one another on the highway that runs from Pegāna to the worlds, or that Kib, the Sender of Life into the Worlds, walks first through the universe, followed by Sish, the Destroyer of Hours, with the death god Mung bringing up the rear. And it is entirely appropriate that there is a beast named Trogool who sits near the edge of the cosmos reading all things from a book. In the manner of the genuine article, this pseudo-mythology touches the subconscious and gains power for doing so. Even if there is no serious religion in the book, any myth, even an invented one, works as a metaphor for existence. In some irrational, obscure way it *fits*. That part of the awareness which perceives things religious responds to it. There is a touch of the otherworldly to it.

What H.P. Lovecraft seemed to admire so much about Dunsany's writing was the detached, cosmic point of view, which reduced mankind to insignificance against the larger picture of things. This is never seen more clearly than in *The Gods of Pegāna*, where all the humans are mites before the gods, who are themselves trivial in the face of **Mana-Yood-Sushai**. (Whose name is always in bold face, perhaps in deference to His majesty.) Dunsany may have been less sincere about this than the misanthropic Lovecraft, who

[9]

PATHWAYS TO ELFLAND

seemed to despise all of our species in the abstract. Thus began what I shall label the "mythic mode" of Dunsany's writing. In his second book, *Time and the Gods* (1906), we are treated to more of the same, only developed to greater length and complexity. This time the pieces are more like conventional short stories, as opposed to the sketches, chants, etc. of *Pegāna*. Once more we encounter Dunsany's hazily-constructed pantheon, and are told stories about the gods and occasional mortals in the manner of the more sophisticated myths of classical antiquity. So, if *The Gods of Pegāna* is primeval and shamanistic, *Time and the Gods* is on the order of Ovid's *Metamorphoses*.

The various tales explain natural phenomena. Typical is "The Legend of the Dawn," in which the Dawn Child casts her golden ball into the sky, only to lose it when it falls beyond the edge of the world and is borne off by Mists, who are described as three shadowy travellers in ragged cloaks. The Dawn Child weeps, and to stop this the North Wind draws his sword of ice from his scabbard of snow, descends beneath the world, battles the Mists, and recovers the ball. In the course of the story the ball is lost again and again and recovered each time by one of the gods representing a force of nature.

Irony is present, as in the account of how the gods walked away from the world in a long line, and when a shepherd who followed them was unable to leave the world, observers took him for a god who had relented and they worshipped him. The shepherd didn't mind a bit.

The style of *Time and the Gods* is for the most part the same as that of *Pegāna*, if a little less ornate in places. The inventions still flow freely, so much so that Dunsany once

[10]

remarked that he didn't feel as if he were inventing at all, but rather relating the "history of lands I had known in forgotten wanderings." The title comes from a line of Swinburne, "Time and the Gods are at strife," which stuck in Dunsany's memory and was only recognized by him years later.

The main difference between this book and its predecessor is that there are some stories in it which deal entirely with human beings. These are the forerunners of those tales of kings and warriors which have had such an influence on writers of "sword and sorcery" fiction over the past seventy years. Still, most of the people in the book are crooked and/or deluded, and their motives tend to be simplistic. A king wants to recover his youth, so he goes with tribute to the Cave of Kai and tries to bribe the creature there into returning his past. Another king leads his army against the castle of Time, only to be defeated by old age when years are hurled against him.

These are the plots of very simple fables, with their morals obvious: you can't recover the past, and you can't stop the flow of time. But Dunsany is not preaching. He is more interested in the poetry of the situations.

A long novelet, "The Journey of the King," was originally written as a separate work, but added at the publisher's request to fill out the book. In it, a king calls on a succession of prophets to tell him about the last journey his soul will take. Each contradicts the previous, but this is hardly something new, since most of the stories in the book contradict one another, or at least bring in gods not previously mentioned. This, however, is to be expected, since mortals can only perceive a small part of the larger whole which is the pantheon of Pegāna.

In the end, one of the prophets announced himself as "THE END," that all-encompassing doom which we encountered in *The Gods of Pegāna*, and the king and the prophet leave the palace and the world, unseen by the others, who have prophesied falsely. Overall, the story doesn't particularly mean anything. It merely *is* for its own sake.

"The Journey of the King" was Dunsany's first story of any length beyond a few pages. It shows what he understood about longer forms at this point and what he didn't, mostly the latter. A long story is not merely a short story stretched out longer. It must have greater complexity and a larger overall structure to accommodate it. But this piece is merely one vignette after another, all strung together by the device of the prophecies. The sum of the parts begins to get a little tedious after a while. He had intended to go on, but when the publisher took what he had written and put it in *Time and the Gods*, Dunsany felt no desire to continue, and admitted enough was enough.

The whole volume represents the climax of the mythic mode and a transition out of it. This is the last time the gods appear by name, although they are rhetorically invoked in later stories merely as "the gods."

Such a development is to be expected because writers must change lest they repeat themselves, and change was very evident indeed by the time of his third collection, *The Sword of Welleran* (1908). Having said all he could about the Gods of Pegāna, he abandoned them and plunged headlong into the heroic or pseudo-heroic phase of his work, coming as close as he ever did to more modern forms of adventure fantasy. Much of his best and most important work belongs to this period.

The title story tells how the ghosts of ancient heroes, guardians of a city, inspire a boy to take up the sword of one of them so the otherwise complacent metropolis might be saved from invading hordes. It is a good story but not a great one, mainly because the characters are types and have little life of their own, and the inventions are too few and too spread apart to make up for this. Far better is "The Fortress Unvanquishable Save for Sacnoth." Dunsany later remarked that this was his most imaginative story, in his opinion, and even he could not account for the degree of invention in it. Indeed, "Fortress" stands out, even among his early fantasies, and is one of the finest short pieces of its type in English. Its basic technique is to pile outrageous image upon outrageous image until the whole makes a kind of sense in its own terms. Thus, when we begin with an evil wizard arriving astride a comet and sending evil dreams to men, it doesn't seem overly preposterous that half-way through the hero kills a monster (which preys on a certain village) by beating it on the nose, and driving it away from that village until it starves; or that in the end the sorcerer can escape an ordinary sword-stroke by lifting his head off his neck and allowing the blade to pass through the gap. The language is elegant, the descriptions clear and vivid; but ultimately the story succeeds on the sheer, staggering power of its inventions. Even Dunsany couldn't quite do such a thing again, but he came close with "The Fall of Babbuklund," in which various travellers tell of a wondrous city to which they are bound. Each relates one particular marvel of the place, all

[13]

PATHWAYS TO ELFLAND

of them progressively more outlandish; but, alas, before they reach their destination the city is destroyed by "the Lord God," who is offended that the Babbuklundians worship idols. Although this deity is never named, he is obviously Jehovah, making this one of the earliest instances of Christian elements in Dunsany's fiction. Surely no run-of-the-mill pagan god would be so intolerant.

The significance of the stories in *The Sword of Welleran* and some of the succeeding volumes is that Dunsany was the first person to adapt the heroic fantasy into the short story form. Usually such tales are *long*. The *Iliad* and the *Odyssey* are long. So are the *Epic of Gilgamesh, Beowulf, Orlando Furioso*, the *Gesar of Ling* epic, and all the rest. The more literary romances of the Middle Ages tend to be of at least moderate length. When Cervantes all but killed the form in a gale of laughter with *Don Quixote*, he took up a lot of wordage doing it. In verse or prose, the same generally holds true; tales of knightly derring-do and adventure in far places go on and on and *on*.

The genre revived in more modern literary forms with William Morris, who, in his college days, did experiment with pseudo-medieval romances at roughly novelet length; but they weren't very good and don't seem to have influenced anybody. His novels, notably *The Well At The World's End*, fared a little better. (And *it* fills two volumes.) Now, the short story as we know it has been around since the late 18th century, but Dunsany seems to have been the first to utilize its techniques to create exquisite miniatures out of the same material so many others used for vast panoramas.

Such stories stand out from what came after them as

EARLY SHORT STORIES

much as they do from their predecessors. Dunsany was the forerunner of the modern "sword and sorcery" writer, but he *wasn't* one himself, at least not in the usual sense. Robert E. Howard's Conan stories are genuinely *barbaric*, the sort of thing primitives might tell while squatting around a campfire, while Dunsany is civilized, witty, and a trifle cynical. The sometimes flippant humor in his work might disorient the reader who is expecting baleful curses and dripping broadswords. Dunsany's stories can have a dreamlike quality; or they can be clever and witty; but it can't be said that they are *exciting*, thrilling, or blood-curdling. They just don't work that way. The fight with the dragon-like creature in "Sacnoth," which Howard would have carried on through pages of breath-taking action, is related briefly and borders on comic.

There is some similarity and acknowledged influence in the case of Fritz Leiber's Fafhrd and the Gray Mouser. Clark Ashton Smith may have followed in Dunsany's footsteps more than he cared to admit—he always insisted his big influences were Bierce and Poe—but the results were often turgid and lifeless. He lacked the stylistic mastery to write as well as Dunsany, and if one doesn't write as well as Dunsany, one can't write like him at all. A typical Dunsany story is like a painting which breaks down into dots and globs of paint if one examines it closely. His plots made sense, and his ideas were often brilliant, but the overall effect depended on the way the stories were told, the right image, the deft turn of a phrase.

H.P. Lovecraft tried to imitate Dunsany after he read *Time and the Gods* in 1919. He was just beginning his adult fiction (as opposed to juvenilia abandoned a decade earlier) at this time and had yet to develop his own voice. So he combined his own ideas with some of Dunsany's and tried to borrow Dunsany's style, and the results were better than they usually are in such cases. Lovecraft's "The Other Gods" is about two prophets who climb a sacred mountain, hoping to see the gods of Earth as they dance there, but instead encounter deities greater and more terrible than any known to mankind. Dunsany had used the idea of gods beyond the ones worshipped by men before in "The Sorrow of the Search" (in *Time and the Gods*), but Lovecraft's deities are far more sinister.

"Celephais," about a man who withdraws entirely into Dreamland and remains there after his physical death, is basically a rewrite of Dunsany's "The Coronation of Mr. Thomas Shap" (from *The Book of Wonder*), although with a somber intensity which makes it better than the original. Dunsany's version is not one of his better efforts, and rather matter-of-factly reports what goes on. Lovecraft's has more feeling.

Most of Lovecraft's other pastiches are inferior, and suffer from Lovecraft's own faults, for all that they may have some slight degree of Dunsany's virtues. The prose tends to be less turgid than that of the other fiction H.P.L. was producing at this time. A short novel, "The Dream Quest of Unknown Kadath," however, bears reading because it carries the Dreamland motif farther than Dunsany ever attempted and does some genuinely innovative things with the material.

Why do so many beginners imitate early Dunsany? What aspects to they imitate? Many, as L. Sprague de Camp once put it, go through a "Dunsany period" the same way mainstream writers go through a Hemingway or a Faulkner period. In such a case, as it was for Lovecraft, this is a passing phase at the beginning of a career, before the writer has found his individual voice. Yet Ursula K. Le Guin, herself a Dunsany admirer who went on to become a major fantasist, warns in her essay, "From Elfland to Poughkeepsie," against Dunsany as The First Terrible Fate that Awaiteth Unwary Beginners in Fantasy, and claims that she has never seen a Dunsany imitation that is more than "a lot of made-up names, some vague descriptions of gorgeous cities and unmentionable dooms, and a great many sentences beginning with 'And'."

While this isn't always the case, as Lovecraft's Dunsanian stories show, there is much truth in the statement. Many such imitations are written, and some are even published, usually in amateur magazines. But a story containing little more than made-up names and repeated uses of "And" stems, most probably, from a lack of understanding of Dunsany's work. It amounts to copying only the most superficial of his mannerisms, and those not very well. If you look through *Time and the Gods* or *The Sword of Welleran* at random, you'll find Dunsany uses what the amateur thinks is "Dunsanian style" far less than he is alleged to. What actually makes his prose so effective is that, archaic or modern, ornate or plain, it always flows smoothly. Recall what he had to say about rhythm. He seems to have had a marvellous ear for sound; and he wasn't above using a common word when a common word would do, quite unlike Clark Ashton Smith, who regurgitated the Oxford Unabridged into print regularly.

Most likely Dunsany realized after a book or two that

archaism, at least extreme archaism, is of limited value and only appropriate for a few types of stories. As he broadened his range, he used the device less and less. The prose of *The Sword of Welleran* is almost modern. The distancing effect of Long Ago and Far Away is achieved by just a few archaic usages sprinkled here and there and simply by the absence of words and phrases unique to the 20th century. In other words, one can get more of an archaic feel by *not* comparing a dragon to a steam engine than by having the characters say, "Forsooth, thou wouldst."

Aside from these mannerisms, which Dunsany himself didn't maintain very long, what is there to copy? Quite a bit. While it must be admitted that any kind of imitation is a sign of literary immaturity and will straightjacket a writer if he doesn't outgrow it, Dunsany is a better master than most. His early fantasies look like exercises in pure style; but they are not, and as soon as the would-be writer realizes this, he may learn something.

The other vital element is *invention*, which is so sorely lacking in those efforts Ms. Le Guin complains about. (Perhaps *imagination* is either lacking or uncultivated in the authors.) There is a vast difference between borrowing someone's techniques and rehashing his ideas. The writers who go through a "Dunsany period" and then have careers of their own tend to be those who express their own ideas with Dunsany's techniques. After all, if you write about the city of Babbuklund or Pegāna or Shard the Pirate, even if you change the names, the story will probably be dull. In a good story of this type, by Dunsany or anyone else, there must be *marvels*, and marvels are less attractive when they are second-hand. Even Dunsany did not often re-use what he had created. Instead he produced new gods, heroes, monsters, cities, and the like in virtually every story.

Sometimes, when a more experienced author tries his hand at it, the results are rather good, doubtless because the writers in these cases have strengths of their own in addition to those taken from Dunsany. Margaret St. Clair's "The Man Who Sold Rope To The Gnoles" achieves delightful humor by updating "How Nuth Would Have Practised His Art Upon The Gnoles" (from *The Book of Wonder*) into the 1950s, complete with a travelling salesman who seems to have stepped out of a television commercial. This, of course, is just a literary joke, not something which can be done more than once. Lin Carter's "The Gods of Niom Parma" (in *Warlocks and Warriors*), ed. de Camp, Putnam 1971) tells of a god from a typically Dunsanian pantheon who becomes a man, decides he likes it, and stays that way. The character is developed in far greater depth than anything in early Dunsany. The style is somewhat less ornate. Carter doesn't string his sentences together with semi-colons or begin with "And" just to let people know he's writing like Dunsany. Few amateur imitators ever get so far.

By contrasting Carter's story with Dunsany, we can see more clearly how Dunsany works. Dunsany was able to write splendid stories without much in the way of characterization or plot, but (beginners please note) a lack of these does not necessarily constitute a virtue. Carter is less inventive than Dunsany and he writes less beautifully, but he produces a good story by taking a Dunsanian framework and doing something original with it. He is telling a *story* in modern terms, which goes from condition A to condition B along the line of a character change.

[19]

PATHWAYS TO ELFLAND

Dunsany didn't always do that. E.F. Bleiler once pointed out while commenting on Ambrose Bierce that it is typical of a Romantic writer (as Dunsany certainly was) to present "archetypal ideas" almost completely without trappings on the grounds that they will seem stronger that way. It is also common for there to be an element of whimsicality or even self-parody. All of this applies to Dunsany as much as it does to Bierce, if not more so.

The early stories are simply works of beauty. They are not allegories. If they say anything, it is that anything which destroys beauty is evil. The wonders in them are presented for their own sake, unencumbered by complicated plots which hinge on psychological change. "The Fall of Babbuklund" exists merely because Dunsany was able to create Babbuklund and describe it in a language befitting its grandeur. That the story is, in a modern sense, pointless is both true and irrelevant. Dunsany was not writing stories in the modern sense, but in his *own* sense. Le Guin points out that "Dunsany mined a narrow vein, but it was all pure ore and it was all his own."

Dunsany is The First Terrible Fate That Awaiteth Beginners in Fantasy because his work lacks so many conventional elements; and the neo-fantasist, not being very skilled at characterization or realistic backgrounds, thinks it is *easy* to write a Dunsany-like story. It isn't. Notice that the constructive borrowings tend to be just that, borrowings of some ideas or techniques for different purposes, rather than attempts to duplicate. The early fantasies are probably the most widely-imitated because they are the most deceptively simple. But to write an effective story within that special "narrow vein" you have to be a genius.

[20]

EARLY SHORT STORIES

You have to be Dunsany.

Curiously, nobody imitates the more earthly stories he wrote in the same period. The myths of the gods and heroes were starting to be supplanted as early as *The Sword of Welleran* by stories equally beautiful, but quite different. "The Highwayman," in that volume, is a perfect example.

It was written in a manner which was to become typical. Sidney Sime, his illustrator, would draw a picture, and Dunsany would construct a tale around it. The illustration shows a ragged corpse dangling in chains from a tree against a somber, grey sky, while three evil-looking men skulk below, bearing a ladder, a lantern, and a sword. Amory in his *Biography* relates how Sime told Dunsany that the three obviously intended to cut out the dead man's heart for use in their sorceries, but Dunsany wrote a milder version in which the trio, thieves and murderers that they are, remain loyal to their hanged comrade and have come to set his soul to rest. They place his body in hallowed ground, in a tomb meant for a bishop, and his soul sails off to Paradise, this being "one sin at which the angels smiled."

This is a story of superstition in a common background, and in subject matter it may be less striking than something like *Time and the Gods*, which is probably why it is less imitated, but the writing is simply superb, so carefully cadenced that we can all but hear the wind blowing and the corpse creaking in its chains on that dismal night.

"The Kith of the Elf-Folk" is the first Dunsany story to have anything to do with Ireland. Dunsany gathered material for it while supposedly campaigning for the election he lost with such panache. He toured factories, and the result was an account of a fairy girl who wants to be mortal, then hates the drudgery of human existence (inside factories, shut off from beauty), and seeks to regain her former state. It's probably too long, and the human sections are a bit limp, as if Dunsany were not really willing or able to write about things which are not beautiful. But in even attempting half-heartedly, he was expanding his range.

"The Ghosts" tends to blend the mythic fantasies with the contemporary ones by giving life and form to abstractions, in this instance the personified sins of a man, which haunt him.

"On the Dry Land" is about a man who almost drowns and dreams that he is viewing all the things and places he loves. That is all there is to the story, but again it is superbly written, and does evoke a mood of longing and nostalgia for the beautiful. Parts of it are highly autobiographical.

After *The Sword of Welleran* came *A Dreamer's Tales* (1910) which contains stories set both nearby and far away. Those set in imaginary lands, or a highly romanticised "East" quite unlike anything which was ever found in the real Orient, tend to be about ordinary people in these places, or at least mortal people. There is a definite pattern in Dunsany, from *The Gods of Pegāna* onward, beginning with the creation of the universe, the remote gods, the earliest kingdoms and prophets, and moving to the more ordinary. In retrospect it looks like an overall plan, but there's no proof it was. Dunsany never said anything to that effect. He was just writing stories, and the progression worked out that way.

"Poltarnees, Beholder of Ocean," is set in a country which is cut off from the sea by arctic wastes, a desert, magic, and mountains. Anybody who goes over the mountains never returns. The answer is of course that the beauty of the sea draws them away.

There really is a Carcassonne in France; and it is a marvellous place, a perfectly preserved medieval walled town with numerous battlements and towers; but in Dunsany's tale of the same name, it becomes a mystical, legendary goal which is never attained. The inspiration for the story came from a letter from a reader, "But he, he never came to Carcassonne," and the plot concerns a king who is inspired by a poet to seek the place, which he does, futilely, for the rest of his life. The story is reminiscent of some of the more human-centered ones in *Time and the Gods*, like "The Sorrow of the Search" and "In the Land of Time."

"In Zaccarath" berates the vanity of man and the ephemeral nature of his works. A prophet tells of the imminent doom of the city, but the King of Zaccarath and his subjects laugh, looking at the splendor around them, insisting the city is eternal. Adroitly, as only he can, Dunsany sums up:

> And only the other day I found a stone that had undoubtedly been a part of Zaccarath, it was three inches long and an inch broad; I saw the edge of it uncovered by the sand. I believe that only three other pieces have been found like it.

(p. 174)

Years later, in *Patches of Sunlight*, Dunsany ventured a guess that the story had been inspired, at least in part, by a ball he had attended in Buckingham Palace and the failure on the part of many people there to realize that war

[23]

PATHWAYS TO ELFLAND

with Germany was growing more likely every day. But of course the situation is as old as, and has obvious parallels in, the handwriting on the wall in Babylon.

Certainly the most famous of the other-worldly tales in the book is "Idle Days on the Yann." William Butler Yeats thought highly of it. In his introduction to *Selections From The Writings of Lord Dunsany*, he wrote, "Had I read 'The Fall of Babbuklund' or 'Idle Days On The Yann' when a boy I had perhaps been changed for better or for worse and looked to that first reading as the creation of my world."

Indeed, the comparison to "Babbuklund" is apt, because both stories are simply exercises in gorgeous invention. "Yann" is longer, and perhaps a little less successful. It was written in anticipation of a trip up the Nile taken in 1908, and is a travelogue of a voyage through the Lands of Wonder, containing many excellent ideas, including the often imitated one of the ivory gate which is cut from a single piece. Unfortunately, it runs on a bit too long; and the limitations of the form start to show. After a while, it is merely rambling, as "The Journey of the King" became.

The other pieces in *A Dreamer's Tales* show more development in what one might call Dunsany's "earthly vein," although, of course, the earth as described by Dunsany could always be expected to come out like nothing anyone else ever lived on. Some of his ventures into remote realms begin in familiar territory. When we visit the fabled city of Bethmoora in the story of the same title, we start our trip in London. After Bethmoora is deserted, perhaps at the command of the evil emperor Thulba Mleen, we are taken to the emperor's court, but get there via a hashish

[24]

dream. ("The Hashish Man" sparked a letter from the
famous occultist Aleister Crowley, who expressed great
interest but observed that the author had obviously not
tried the drug, since he didn't get the spatial distortions
right. He sent along some pornographic magazines. Dunsany's reply is not known. He and Beatrice were both taken
aback, no doubt.)

Two of the most interesting items transform the utterly
ordinary into the marvellous. "Blagdaross" is another *tour-
de-force* of invention, in which things deliberately chosen
for their insignificance, an old cork, a spent match, a
junked rocking horse Dunsany had seen from the window
of a train, tell their stories. The results are brilliant, but
even more unlikely was the source of inspiration for
"Where The Tides Ebb and Flow," one of his most unusual
efforts. Allegedly it was done on a dare, to see if he really
could write a story about the mud at the bottom of the
Thames. In any case, he made the observation that the
mud at low tide had "a certain strangeness about it which
might be material for prose." He was far away from the
Thames, in Rome, when the idea actually began to take
shape. He began:

> I dreamt that I had done a horrible thing, so that
> burial was denied me either in soil or sea, neither
> could there be any hell for me.
> I waited for some hours, knowing this. Then my
> friends came for me, and slew me secretly and with
> ancient rite, and lit great tapers, and carried me away.
> (p. 40)

PATHWAYS TO ELFLAND

The story is darker and gloomier than most of Dunsany's work; and at times it reads more like Kafka than Dunsany, save that the language is a lot richer than Kafka's tends to be in translation. The narrator has violated the rules of a secret society and can find no respite from them even after death. Generations of the membership keep digging up his bones each time he is buried, so his soul can never rest. Even when a storm scatters his remains to far isles, the tides inexorably bring them back to the mud by the edge of the Thames. At last, when all mankind has passed away and the world has reverted to nature, the curse is broken. "He has sinned against man," say the birds. "It is not our quarrel." So they lift his spirit up to heaven.

This borders on surrealism, save that it makes too much obvious sense. It isn't allegorical, strictly speaking, since nothing represents more than it is; but it does possess a larger meaning and a genuine sense of alienation. The entire narrative is from the viewpoint of the corpse. He is a lonely outsider watching the flotsam of the world drift by. He learns slowly what the king of Zaccarath learned in one fell swoop, that human things are less important and less lasting than nature. The story is rich in atmosphere. It is an act even Dunsany found hard to follow. Because it is so unlike his other work, it tends to be over-looked, but it is one of the best fantasy short stories in English.

Another innovative item was a nasty little tale called "Poor Old Bill," which Dunsany later compared with Poe. It's about a crew of mutinous sailors who maroon their captain, only to receive his curse. Their ship can never touch land while he is alive. Supplies run out and eventually the sailors eat one another, until only the narrator remains.

In technique, the story is interesting for two reasons. First, it is the earliest attempt to tell a story second-hand, in conversation within a framework. Dunsany later became a master of this.

Second, it is an attempt to tell the story in dialect. It may not sound like the way real sailors talk, but we are willing to believe that *this* sailor, who suffered a curse of a sorcerer captain on a distant ocean over a hundred years before he tells about it, may very well relate his adventures like this:

> And these two used to watch one another night and day, when Dick was gone and no one else was left to them. And at last Poor Old Bill fell down in a faint and lay there for an hour. Then Jakes came up to him slowly with his knife, and there makes a stab at poor old Bill as he lies there on the deck. And poor old Bill caught hold of him by the wrist, and put his knife into him twice to make quite sure, although it spoiled the best part of the meat. Then poor old Bill was all alone at sea.
>
> (p. 136)

Curious, at least, is "The Day of the Poll." This is Dunsany's first non-fantasy. It's about a poet who takes a voter out into the fields on election day, and shows him a beauty more important than voting. Some of this might be a sour grapes reaction to Dunsany's own brief excursion into politics, but not much. One gets the distinct impression he thought it just as well that he'd lost. His interests were

[27]

elsewhere.

The last truly great book of this period, judged by many to be the finest, was *The Book of Wonder* (1912). This time virtually all the stories are written around Sime drawings. Sime, apparently, had been complaining that he was being given too little suitable material to illustrate, so Dunsany accommodated him.

One shows a sinister old woman sitting at the foot of a tree made out of what seems to be shiny stone studded with stars. Beside her is an abyss, and a swordsman is crossing it on a bridge made from a fallen tree. An enormous glowing diamond is on the bridge at his feet. In the background are enormous spiderwebs and more trees, one with a lighted window in it, a door with steps, and a corpse hanging from either side. The title of the picture is "The Ominous Cough," and Dunsany begins "The Distressing Tale of Thangobrind the Jeweler" with the lines:

> When Thangobrind the Jeweler heard the ominous cough, he turned at once upon that narrow way. A thief was he, of very high repute, being patronised by the lofty and the elect, for he stole nothing smaller than Moomoo's egg, and in all his life stole only four kinds of stone—the ruby, the diamond, the emerald, and the sapphire; and, as jewelers go, his honesty was great.
>
> (p. 11)

The stone Thangobrind seeks this time is Dead Man's Diamond, which is found in the lap of the spider-idol Hlo-Hlo, and "was often stolen, but it had a knack of coming

back again into the lap of Hlo-Hlo." Of course Thangobrind does not realise that the ominous cough is a warning
until much too late.

The Book of Wonder differs greatly in tone from the earlier
collections. H.P. Lovecraft thought the increased irony and
humor meant that Dunsany had sold out to the crass world
of literary fashion, but this is not the case. Chances are,
Lovecraft took the early stories more seriously than Dunsany did. And recall the Bleiler observation on Romantics,
or, perhaps we should say, late Romantics. The element of
self-parody, of not quite being able to believe in the pure
and the beautiful even as one wrote about it, is common
to the work of many of the Romantic writers of the turn
of the century. Wilde deliberately set out to create beauty
in his fairy tales and his poems (many of those all but
plagiarized from another romantic, William Morris) and
the result usually had a touch of irony at the very least.
James Branch Cabell, the one great romantic fantasist in
America contemporary with Dunsany, stated that he
wanted to write "beautifully of beautiful things," but usually ended up lampooning the same, though with a sub-
dued feeling of sadness that the world can't be so ideal.
Anatole France did the same thing at times. So Dunsany's
greater use of irony and even satire in his otherwise
dreamy and unworldly fantasies is not a phenomenon limited to one author. But he was never one to conform to
fashion (the fashionable thing would have been to write
about traditional Irish legendry, the way Yeats and James
Stephens did), so it seems likely that he merely took this
new emphasis for granted, and perhaps perceived it only
as that, a slight shift in emphasis, rather than a wholesale

change. After all, weren't his stories as filled with marvels as before?

He even developed a new marvel which was to become a major concept in his work: the edge of the world. The subtitle of the book is "A Chronicle of Little Adventures at the Edge of the World." This is the edge of *our* world. The cosmos of it includes London; but the farther away one goes from familiar places, the more fabulous the geography becomes. At last, the Earth ends with a sheer drop into an abyss of mist and stars. Dunsany can't resist gleefully tossing a few characters over the brink, but this isn't the most dreadful fate in store for the unwary in that vicinity. The unfortunate Slith, Slorg, and Sippy, in "Probable Adventure of the Three Literary Men," come to the Edge to steal the Golden Box, wherein are found the greatest poems ever written. They are caught by the guardian of the box, who remains undescribed, but we are told that it is the *wisest* of the three who takes the easy way out by jumping into infinity.

Most resembling a traditional fairy tale, or at least a parody thereof, is "The Hoard of The Gibbelins," in which a knight persuades a dragon to carry him to the Edge of the World, arguing that dragons never win against knights in these stories, and if he wants to go on eating maidens, he'd better cooperate. Once the destination is reached the allegedly noble knight, whose real motivation is greed, tries to make off with the fabulous hoard of the Gibbelins, beings who eat "nothing less good than man." All seems to be going smoothly until:

And, without a word, *or even smiling*, they neatly

hanged him on the outer wall—and the tale is one of those that have not a happy ending.

(p. 83)

The twist ending is one of Dunsany's best. It snaps like a trap on a sly turn of phrase before the reader scarcely notices the story is over. The story itself is less good, being a trifle self-conscious and artificial. Having the characters aware that encounters between knights and dragons always end in a traditional way is perhaps carrying the irony a little too far.

Not all the stories are about people stealing things from supernatural creatures and meeting dooms mentionable or otherwise. Also included are tales like those in the earlier collections, notably "How One Came, As Was Foretold, to the Cuty of Never" and "The Bride of the Man-Horse;" "Chu-Bu and Sheemish," which is about the disastrous consequences of a feud between two petty idols; the aforementioned "The Coronation of Mr. Thomas Shap," which was probably reworked by Lovecraft because he didn't like the ironic deflation of having the dreamer carted off to the booby-hatch at the end; "The Wonderful Window," a non-humorous story about a world seen through a magic window (one can't be sure if this is the first instance of such in fantasy fiction, but those windows have been turning up with some frequency ever since); and several others. The least satisfactory are those which merely explain what is going on in the picture, such as "The House of the Sphinx." The best of them are splendid, quite unlike *A Dreamer's Tales* or *The Sword of Welleran*, but good in their own right.

[31]

PATHWAYS TO ELFLAND

After *The Book of Wonder* Dunsany's imagination began to run down, and even he was hard pressed to come up with more marvels. *The Last Book of Wonder*, published in 1916 but containing material written before World War I, is much weaker than the volumes preceding it. There are some excellent tales included, certainly; but the significant thing is that the inferior ones tend to be those in the Edge of the World mode. This was to become a characteristic pattern. Dunsany would begin well in any vein, writing his best stories of the type near the beginning, maintain a high level of quality for a while, and then fall off to the point of utter exhaustion. The quality of execution does not decline, but the stories become too contrived and insubstantial, frequently promising great things and delivering nothing.

For example, "How Plash-Goo Came to the Land of None's Desire" tells of a giant who is thrown over the Edge of the World. He falls for days, and at last a country appears below. This is called the Land of None's Desire because no one wishes to fall there and perish on impact. The writer seems to be saying "I fooled you!" After a few repetitions the reader ceases to be fooled and says "So what?" Perhaps Dunsany was aware, because "Why the Milkman Shudders When He Sees the Dawn" is a parody of the whole gimmick. It drew laughs when Lovecraft heard it read in Boston in 1919, but in the context of the book it seems only slightly more preposterous than most.

The best stories in *The Last Book of Wonder* explore new areas. They are set, not in dreamland, but in fabulous versions of our own world. "A Tale of Land and Sea" is a companion to "The Loot of Bombasharna" in *The Book*

of Wonder and goes far beyond it, telling how Shard the
Pirate and the men of the bad ship *Desperate Lark* escape
the collected navies of Europe by putting the vessel on
wheels and sailing across Africa. The story is told with
tongue-in-cheek, but without slipping into outright parody. "Thirteen At The Table" is the start of a new trend.
It contains the first of the hunting scenes which would
grow longer and longer, especially in the novels, until they
threatened to drag everything to a halt. Here the description of a fox hunt is short and interesting, and at the end
of it the hero comes to a house and unwittingly releases
the place from a curse, since his bad manners have offended the ghosts who periodically dine there.

"The Exiles' Club" bids farewell to the gods. The narrator comes to a club where all the waiters are former
kings. Upstairs are the members, also exiles, presumably
former gods.

And then the old gods go out, the Christian Devil comes
in. Present are two very fine stories of pacts with the Ad-
versary: "The Three Infernal Jokes" is about a man who
bargains for three jokes, which literally make people die
laughing. "The Three Sailors' Gambit" is the supernatural
chess story to end all supernatural chess stories. Three
sailors have obtained from His Infernal Majesty a crystal
ball which will tell them how to win at chess. They stretch
its ability a bit too far by going against a master with only
a king and a row of pawns.

These are tall tales, not wonder tales; and they showed
what was to come, just as the tired Edge-of-the-World ones
showed what was left behind. Dunsany's style and approach were changing. There is no attempt at a sense of

PATHWAYS TO ELFLAND

"long ago and far away" in something like "The Three Sailors' Gambit." He is writing in a sprightly, modern style about unusual things in the here and now, in a manner which John Collier, Stephen Vincent Benét, Mark Van Doren (*The Witch of Ramoth*), and others would use to great success decades later.

One more book of the early "wonder" group appeared, also containing pre-war stories, although it was not published until 1919. *Tales of Three Hemispheres* may be better than some people's best, but much of it is second rate Dunsany. Many of the stories are as superficial as the worst in *The Last Book of Wonder*, and the few in the newer, modern vein aren't very good either. "The Sack of Emeralds" has a few moments of effective atmosphere. "How the Office of Postman Fell Vacant in Otford-under-the-Wold" is up to the level of the best, or nearly so, mixing irony and menace deftly. The others can pretty well be ignored, save for "The Shop on Go-By Street" and "The Avenger of Perdóndaris," both of which are sequels to "Idle Days On The Yann." In 1911 the three had been published in *The Irish Review* under the collective title "Beyond the Fields We Know," and as such they appear in *Three Hemispheres*, complete with a duplication of "Yann" from *A Dreamer's Tales*. The two new stories are top-drawer Dunsany, as beautiful and inventive as the original, but more coherent, suggesting that at last Dunsany was learning how to write novelettes rather than padded short-stories. "Go-By Street" does interesting things with the different time-rates in Dreamland and the waking world. It made quite an impression on Lovecraft, who made a note about it in his *Commonplace Book* and borrowed much from it, particularly the

[34]

" 'Why! you will beat me yet.' "
"A Losing Game"

[36]

idea of Dreamland as a definite place or alternate plane of existence. "The Avenger of Perdóndaris" introduces the hunter who slays the beasts with tusks so huge one can carve city gates out of them. This time one of the tusks, whole, is used as a bridge. Alas that post-war economy precluded any Sime illustrations. One wonders what he could have done with such a scene. Happily, Tim Kirk executed it beautifully in the 1976 Owlswick Press reprint.

Actually, *Tales of Three Hemispheres* is not as bad as it sounds. If most of the stories are trivial, they are also short and get out of the way quickly. The better ones are longer. "Otford" and "Beyond The Fields We Know" make up more than half the total wordage. The book is worth reading for them alone.

Another product of the pre-war period was *Fifty-One Tales*, published in 1915. The contents date back to 1908, the time of *A Dreamer's Tales* and *The Sword of Welleran*, but they are not as good as those. All are experiments with the short-short story, none being more than about three hundred words long. An effective tale of such brevity is one of the most difficult of all prose forms, comparable to haiku in verse. Sure, anybody can write a poem that looks like a haiku, and anyone can write a story three paragraphs long, but how many are *any good*? Dunsany only proved by the effort that he wasn't quite up to it either. The stories are short fables, allegories (not moralistic, but making points with obviously symbolic figures), and an occasional joke. All are quite readable, but few are memorable. One gets through the book quickly because there is always another tale at hand if the last was unsatisfactory. Dunsany seldom tried this form later, and was

[37]

never distinguished at it.

As the first period of Dunsany's writing came to an end, so did an era, with appalling suddenness, in August of 1914. The First World War was a traumatic experience for him, and a definite dividing line in his career. In brief, the real world with all its grimness hit him in the face. He served some time in the trenches, and his friends were slaughtered wholesale. His autobiographies are sprinkled with references to this or that friendship which lasted "until 1914." The horror of this, in addition to the Irish Easter Rebellion of 1916, in which Dunsany was wounded and his castle threatened, made it difficult to write frivolous, escapist fantasy.

His only books produced during the war were two collections of short sketches, *Tales of War* (1918) and *Unhappy Far-Off Things* (1919). They are quite enlightened by the standards of the British propaganda of the time, with its boiled Belgian babies and human fat used to oil German machines, but still they were propaganda first, and art only incidentally. It would have been quite possible for a German author to have written the same things. (Indeed, one of Dunsany's friends once mentioned to a German prisoner that the Germans were the Huns threatening civilization, and the prisoner replied that the British were.) A modern reader is less impressed with what Dunsany has to say about the rightness of the Cause, the heroism of Allied soldiers, or the personal guilt of the Kaiser, than the melancholy meditations on the destruction of the beautiful, the descriptions of landscapes rendered unrecognizable by shell fire, and even the admission that the Germans are honest people deluded by their leaders, rather than blood-thirsty barbarians. One item, "The Road," is a tribute to a friend killed while working on a road crew. *Unhappy Far-Off Things*, published just as the war was ending, begins with a Dirge of Victory. Of course, since they were propaganda, the pieces tend to be vague and evasive when dealing with the immediate horrors of war, lest they dispirit the public. One only need compare these two books with *All Quiet on the Western Front* to see why they didn't survive beyond their time.

Plays

When reading this chapter, remember that I have never seen a Dunsany play performed. They are simply not put on anymore, at least not professionally, so one can only guess what they would be like on the stage. Frequently a play "plays" far differently than it reads. Bierstadt's *Dunsany the Dramatist* contains photos of scenes from some of the early productions, which give the impression that, typical of their era, they were elaborate, even ponderous affairs, filled with rigid, spectacular sets and ornate costumes. But only the murky glass of imagination can tell us how the lines were delivered, what the direction was like, or how good the acting was.

Dunsany became a dramatist suddenly one afternoon in the spring of 1909. This was the heyday of the self-proclaimed Irish Renaissance, when the Abbey Theatre in Dublin was getting into its stride, and Yeats and Lady Gregory were doing their best to create a national dramatic literature. They wrote plays themselves, and recruited new Irish writers, giving them a chance to get their plays before the public. Their biggest find was J.M. Synge. One of their lesser ones was Dunsany.

That afternoon in question, Yeats asked Dunsany to write a play. Dunsany had done a drawing which caught Yeats' eye, and the latter asked, "Why don't you make a play out of it?" Dunsany replied that he didn't write plays. This was true. Up to then, he hadn't. "Well," said Yeats, "I guess I'll have to get someone else to do it."

At that, Dunsany accepted the challenge. On March 23, 1909, he wrote *The Glittering Gate*, a one-acter about two burglars who pick the lock to the gates of Heaven only to find a starry abyss on the other side. He showed it to Yeats, who then gave him the only lesson in the art of play construction he ever recieved. To hold the audience's attention while the lock was being picked, Yeats suggested, there had to be something else going on. A few lines of dialogue would do. So Dunsany added some dialogue, having the burglars speculate about what they expect to find in Heaven. This intensifies the effect when they discover there is no Heaven, and the theatre fills with thunderous laughter from the depths of the cosmos.

The play was performed at the Abbey on April 29, 1909, and later in Manchester, Belfast, and London. It reached New York in 1915. The reviews were mostly lukewarm, a few favorable, and some with objections on religious and other grounds. It went over well enough with audiences, and Dunsany's dramatic career was launched. His apprenticeship consisted of nothing more than the conversation with Yeats, and those few lines of additional dialogue were about the only revision he ever made. He knew little of the practical mechanics of stagecraft, but seemed to have an

[41]

instinctive grasp of what could be done. At least nothing he turned out was beyond the limits of the players at the Abbey. One important bit of advice Yeats had given him was that surprise is the most important element of drama, and he took this to heart. Nearly all his early plays hinge at least partially on surprise. Besides that, he followed no set of rules. In his *Donellan Lectures* and "The Carving of the Ivory," one of a series of lectures published by the University of Pennsylvania in 1928, he argued that there were no secret techniques or formulas to be memorized, even if some dramatists did bow to convention. It had once occurred to him to study the art of play construction, so he bought a book on the subject. He read on the first page how certain basics had been the same for "all from Aeschylus to Lord Dunsany" and read no further.

His second play was *King Argimenes and the Unknown Warrior*, in two acts this time, written, appropriately enough, in two days, February 22-23, 1910. It was performed at the Abbey in January of 1911, published in *The Irish Review* that September, and ultimately became one of his best-known dramatic works. The conception of the play began with the image of a king in rags, not merely gnawing on a bone, but relishing it. From this came the story of King Argimenes, a deposed ruler reduced to slavery, who finds the sword of an ancient warrior while working in the fields, and with it leads the other slaves to revolt, capturing the throne of his oppressor, King Darniak. The final confirmation of his recovered dignity comes when word is brought that Darniak's dog has died. His followers drool over the prospect of fresh bones, but Argimenes orders the beast buried. He won't lower himself to eating bones anymore.

King Argimenes brings to the stage the material of Dunsany's stories of the same period. It is a quasi-Oriental extravaganza, dealing with imaginary lands, kings, and gods. It particularly resembles "The Sword of Welleran" with the motif of a sword inspiring people to valor. His writing was as good as ever, but the play left his weaknesses more visible than the stories did.

His strengths, as always, were his soaring imagination and his beautiful style. In drama he added an easy use of situation and an ear for dialogue, though usually of the poetical and lofty variety, rather than realistic. But sometimes, perhaps because he hadn't studied stagecraft, he would attempt more than the medium would bear. Also, he failed to develop his characters.

Individual human beings are never the focus of interest in the early plays. On the basis of the first few, Bierstadt concluded that Dunsany's art was wholly detached from human affairs, lofty and ethereal. He was only half correct. Dunsany was more interested in broad types than in individuals with unique quirks; and he populated his plays with prophets, kings, beggars, and soldiers, all of whom were pretty well interchangeable. This is also true of his early stories, but there it mattered less. In a story, the author's viewpoint can take over. The prose can be remote. Everything can be described from a distance and seen as part of a larger pattern. But on stage the focus is on the characters. Yeats mentioned a play he had received which contained a couple of paragraphs of flowery language, all of which amounted to "Sun sets, left."

Consequently, the trend of the times was toward greater

characterization. The English stage had suddenly burst to life ten years earlier, after a century of sleep; and modern drama was being born. From the 1860s onward, Ibsen's vastly influential works had delved deeper and deeper into the recesses of the human mind. A play like *Hedda Gabler* works not on the basis of plot, but by creating the inescapable presence of a real woman, about whom the audience cares deeply. But Dunsany defined drama in terms of event. The material a dramatist worked with was dialogue, but the essence of a play to him was a series of events which are revealed in a flash to be the inevitable workings of fate. The surprise recommended by Yeats had become "the surprise of truth." In "The Carving of the Ivory" Dunsany states:

> . . . when the climax of the play is reached, the first emotion of the audience is astonishment, and the second emotion, rapidly following, is, "Why, of course."
>
> (p.61)

Such a preoccupation with fate is classically Greek, which is only natural since Dunsany was influenced more by the ancient Greek dramatists than anyone else. His use of types, rather than individuals, is also something he picked up from the Greeks. What do we really know about Oedipus, save that he is a wise and clever king plagued with a bad temper, whose parents tried to evade the decrees of fate? The inner neuroses of the character don't seem to have interested Sophocles. He was writing about the conflict between man, fate, and the gods, not that between man and his inner nature. Dunsany was doing the same,

[44]

and in this he was led into a trap.

His current obscurity as a playwright is due to more than his being out of step with his times. It isn't at all surprising that Dunsany, with his education and interests, went back to classical roots. There was virtually no significant English drama after Sheridan and before the middle 1890s, so Dunsany had to either do what his contemporaries were doing or go back well before his lifetime for models. Restoration comedy would hardly have suited. He appreciated the great Elizabethans, and doubtless borrowed from them; but they weren't what he wanted either.

Fine, but a little bit of inner nature wouldn't have hurt. If his characters had had a little more to them, the plays would have been all that much richer. *Macbeth* is a play of man against fate, but it is also one of character. If Dunsany had made his characters live, fate would have been knocking down a real human being, in whom the audience had some emotional stake, and this would have been more powerful than the same actions with stick men. Perhaps a great actor could have pulled it off, and for all anyone today knows, perhaps one did, but the characters don't seem very three-dimensional when one reads the script. Shakespeare's do. So do Shaw's. So do Ibsen's. All Dunsany seems to be doing is providing characters who don't do anything a real person wouldn't in a given circumstance. The rapid unfolding of events, the novelty, and the language make *King Argimenes* a good play; but alone they failed to make it a great one.

The element of surprise, or really the lack thereof, also presents a problem. The king's revolt and triumph come much too easily, without complications. Bierstadt sug-

[45]

PATHWAYS TO ELFLAND

gested that the order of events should have been changed. As it is, the play starts with the finding of the sword, switches to a court scene in which Darniak ignores prophecies of doom, then carries the revolt to its conclusion. He wanted the court scene at the beginning, which would have made things more direct, without a promise of a surprise so the audience won't be disappointed when no surprise is delivered (unless you want to count Argimenes's refusal to eat dog bones). In any case, the play is mostly action, wit, and pageantry. It is entertaining, but not earthshattering. Years later Dunsany referred to it as being "full of flaws." It provided some of the background for Fletcher Pratt's 1948 fantasy classic, *The Well of the Unicorn*, in which the action took place in the same universe several generations after Argimenes's revolt.

In the summer of 1910 Dunsany began a play in three acts, *The Gods of the Mountain*. It premiered at the Haymarket Theatre in London on June 1, 1911, and ran for three months with the house packed. Its success spurred Yeats and Lady Gregory to bring *King Argimenes* to London, where it was performed at the Court Theatre.

The Gods of the Mountain is set in "the East," in a country of idolaters. By clever ruses, a group of beggars convince the people of a city that they are really the jade gods which sit atop a nearby mountain, come among men in human form. The idea, of course, is to live royally off the sacrifices offered to them. Unfortunately the real gods take a dim view of this, enter the city, and turn the beggars to stone; the final irony being that the people take this as proof that the beggars really were gods, now reverted to their original form.

[46]

The play is filled with clever, sometimes terrifying touches, such as the scene in which the townsmen send messengers to the hills to see if the gods are still there, and learn they are *gone*. Only Agmar, the leader of the beggars, and the audience know what dreadful things are in store when the citizens begin to plead with the impostors not to go about in their "natural" guise, for "rock should not walk in the evening." Suspense builds marvellously, until heavy footsteps are heard approaching and Dunsany makes a serious technical blunder.

His stage directions at this point read:

> The stony boots come on. Enter in single file through door in right of back, a procession of seven green men, even hands and faces are green.
>
> (*Five Plays*, p.36)

The mistake is, of course, to bring the gods on stage. We don't notice it as much when reading the play, but every critic who saw it seems to have complained that when the gods entered it was evident they were only actors in makeup, not gods at all. Since Dunsany had none of the genuine article to deliver, he would have done better to have left the appearance of the gods to the audience's imagination. The problem is very similar to that of the horror movie in which the monster is obviously a man in a rubber suit.

Aside from this, the play is an improvement over *Argimenes* in every way. The characters aren't drawn in great detail, but they are more clearly defined. The plot contains complications and genuine surprises. The ending is a great

[47]

surprise, which we see coming only very shortly before it arrives. And after it does, it seems quite fitting, and the audience, according to Dunsany's dictum, says, "why, of course."

His theatrical career now in full swing, he wrote several more plays at his usual rapid pace. First he tried a short melodrama, *The Murderers*, which must not have been very successful. It was performed only a very few times, and has never been published. *The Golden Doom* did a lot better.

Again the setting is the East, but now vaguely connected with history, "some while before the fall of Babylon." A child writes a nonsense verse on the King's door in gold, and it is taken to be a divine message. Prophets interpret the lines and wail of doom. Ultimately the King sacrifices his pride, symbolized by his crown, so that the city might be spared. The child, who had come to the door to ask the King for a pretty golden hoop, is satisfied. The blatant point is that in the overall scheme of things the fate of a kingdom and the whim of a child are the same.

The play fits together seamlessly. It is entertaining to read and proved to be quite successful on the stage, even if the press was unenthusiastic. There is little to be said against *The Golden Doom*. If it seems unsatisfactory in any way, what you really want is a different play.

On the heels of this came *The Tents of the Arabs*, a two-act play about a king of an Arab country who goes out to live among the nomads, falls in love with a nomad woman, and allows himself to be impersonated when it is time for him to return to the capital. The play has no fantastic elements, save that the Arabs are romanticised to the point of being virtually unrecognizable, rather the way the Jap-

anese are in *The Mikado*. This was not done out of ignorance, because by this time Dunsany had visited North
Africa and become acquainted with many Arabs; but one
can't help but feel it might have seemed a bit more plausible
if set in medieval Europe against the background of the
courtly love tradition. Dunsany, however, doubtless would
have argued that when he wrote, he did so from his imagination, and his imagination was not about to be tied down
by mere geographical and cultural realities.

Next came what is probably his finest play, *The Laughter
of the Gods*, written on January 29th and February 2nd and
3rd, 1911, but not performed or published until after the
war. The story is fantasy; and as in his best prose tales, the
elements of wonder, humor, and supernatural terror are
perfectly balanced.

King Karnos and his courtiers move to the jungle city
of Thek, much to the dismay of their wives, who consider
tł e capital more fashionable. The wives want to leave, but
the husbands enjoy the hunting too much and won't. So
the wives conspire and force a prophet to proclaim falsely
that the gods have revealed to him that they will destroy
Thek if the King does not leave. While the prophet be-
moans the fact he has lied in the name of the gods, the
King decides to stay, since the gods have not destroyed a
city in so long he doubts they do that sort of thing anymore.
If they don't, he will execute the prophet for lying. In the
end the gods call the King's bluff, vindicating their truth-
fulness, but unlike the walking idols of *The Gods of the
Mountain*, they never appear, and their mocking laughter
from offstage is the more terrible for it.

Once again Dunsany calls for a spectacle, seemingly

more appropriate for Cecil B. DeMille than the live stage, but he gets away with it. Probably the on-stage destruction of Thek was not even the splashiest spectacle of the year. One should recall that theatrical productions in the teens and twenties tended to have larger budgets than those of today. Sets were more elaborate. Cutting corners by having a bare stage and pretending to be avant-garde was unheard of. Audiences expected to *see* something. Therefore this passage isn't at all unreasonable:

> KING KARNOS.
> The jungle is sinking! It has fallen into the earth!
> [*The Queen smiles a little, holding his hand.*]
> The city is falling in! The houses are rolling towards us!
> [*Thunder off.*]
> ICTHARION.
> They are coming like a wave and a darkness is coming with them.
> [*Loud and prolonged thunder. Flashes of red light and then total blackness. A little light comes back, showing recumbent figures. The Prophet's back is broken, but he raises the forepart of his body for a moment.*]
> VOICE-OF-THE-GODS
> [*Triumphantly.*]
> They have not lied!
> (*Plays of Gods and Men*, p. 129)

Come to think of it, this would have been relatively easy to stage. About the same time there was a version of *Ben Hur*, complete with on-stage chariot races with real horses and the naval battle done with stagehands flapping huge draperies to simulate the ocean!

Since *The Laughter of the Gods* was not to be staged until 1919 and *King Argimenes* was a success, it was only logical that Dunsany should try to repeat the latter. He did, but in doing so he repeated its central mistake also.

A Night at an Inn brought a walking idol clunking on stage again. This time the plot is rather like that of Wilkie Collins's *The Moonstone*. English rogues have stolen the jeweled eye of a Hindu idol and are pursued by vengeful priests, each of whom is dispatched without much difficulty. Where Collins developed his story into detection, Dunsany went for the supernatural. The Englishmen think themselves safe, only to find themselves face to face with the god Klesh himself. Each meets a nameless doom. At least Dunsany had enough sense to leave that much off stage. The thieves are irresistibly called away at the end, and the final scene is effective. But otherwise the stage direction "enter a hideous idol" is the man-in-the-rubber-suit problem all over again.

The play is passable melodrama, which went on to greater success than it really deserved, but when one thinks about it, the plot makes little sense. If the priests brought Klesh to England with them, why did they not send him/it in first, or all attack together, rather than be killed off one at a time? If they did *not*, then not only can the idol walk, but it can also transport itself instantaneously over great distances, which may be too much for the audience to accept all at once. And if it can do that, why bother to send priests at all? It would be more satisfying to have the idol move slowly, relentlessly; and have it show up years later, dripping and covered with seaweed, when the robbers are wealthy and respectable. It is only because of the quick pace, the shortness of the play (one act), and the constant suspense that one doesn't notice these things until afterwards.

The modern setting was a first for Dunsany, and something to be repeated. In 1912 he wrote a non-fantasy social comedy, *The Lost Silk Hat*, which was produced in Manchester the following spring.

Bierstadt compared it to *The Importance of Being Earnest*, and the point is valid. It is the same kind of play, falling short of Wilde's only by degree. It may be not as devastatingly witty, but it thrusts in the same direction. In it, a well-dressed man on a fashionable London street accosts a passing laborer, asking him to come up with an excuse to enter a certain house and recover the gentleman's hat. The laborer suspects a crime and refuses. A clerk finds the proposal simply improper. A poet is more cooperative in theory; but since he refuses to indulge in anything as inartistic as clock-winding or piano-tuning, he also refuses. The truth comes out. The young man has quarrelled with his beloved, run off to die in a foreign war, but forgotten his hat. The poet thinks this a splendidly romantic idea, and warns the lover not to go back, lest he accidentally apologize and ruin the whole thing. But he realizes that the poet is a trifle too eager to have him laid in an unmarked grave and rendered a fit subject for poetry, so he goes back and apologizes. "They're going to kill romance," moans the poet.

The play is, of course, a trifle. Critics found it pleasant, but no more. The poet's refusal to do anything inartistic is a contrivance. Otherwise he would have been willing to get the man's hat, if only to assure that he would go off to the wars and inspire great poetry. The plot is another one of those whose holes begin to show at a second glance. *The Lost Silk Hat* never did well commercially. It was not performed in London or anywhere in America until much later, even though it eventually turned up in such diverse places as China and Russia. It is certainly a minor work.

The *major* work of the year, which occupied Dunsany off and on between April and July, was *Alexander*, his first four-act play. It was originally supposed to be a collaboration with Padraic Colum, but before Colum could get more than a few pages done Dunsany was well into the project, and the two decided Dunsany should write it alone.

Dunsany also had a good reason to be wary of collaboration. He had often encountered prejudice against his work because he was a peer. A lord, said the conventional wisdom of the day, could never be more than a dilettante, a rich idler incapable of turning out anything worthwhile. At one point he had even considered changing his byline to Edward Plunkett, but decided against it, lest he lose what readers he had. If a play appeared as by Lord Dunsany and Padraic Colum, critics and the public would assume Colum (an excellent author in his own right) had written it all, and they might begin to suspect that he ghosted the rest of Dunsany's work as well. So it was just as well that they did not collaborate.

Alexander is a very Greek play, not only for its ancient Greek subject matter, but in its basic construction. Again, in accordance with Dunsany's theory of drama, we have an overview of man, the gods, and the workings of fate.

PATHWAYS TO ELFLAND

Alexander is more a type than an individual, the greatest of all conquerors, a classic over-reacher like Marlowe's Tamberlaine (and equally uninteresting). Apollo, in the guise of an old man, stands in for the gods as Alexander's advisor from boyhood onward. The Fates appear in interludes, deliberately spinning the hero's thread stronger and finer than most. But when he oversteps his bounds, one of the Sisters reaches for the shears.

Alexander, like all classic tragic characters, makes a big mistake and spends the rest of the play paying for it. Flatterers with names like Sycophantes and Psuestes convince him that he should dismiss his advisor (Apollo); and he does, forsaking the help of the gods. Then, convinced that his success is due to his own divine nature, he kills his best friend in an argument over the matter. In deep mourning, he neglects his worldly duties and breaks off the beginnings of a love affair with the Queen of the Amazons. After conquering India, he dies as history tells us he did, fulfilling the prophecy that he would be brought as low as the statue of Xerxes he overthrew while burning Persepolis in Act I. His generals then set to haggling over the division of the empire, without even bothering to bury the corpse, which lies unattended until the Amazon Queen, who truly loved Alexander, comes to claim it.

Somehow the play never quite jells. It is a serious shortcoming that Alexander has so little personality. Much of the interest in a play about a famous person is how the author brings that figure to life. One of Shaw's great triumphs in *Caesar and Cleopatra* was making Caesar a kindly and worldly-wise old man with a sense of humor. Of course Dunsany was more concerned with the gods and fate, but this may be a case of a writer choosing the wrong goal. The fact that he did not develop Alexander's character does not prove him incapable of developing character, but it doesn't help the play much either. Where we might have had genuine tragedy, we get a historical pageant mixed with mildly interesting fantasy. Unfortunately Alexander in Persepolis is not King Karnos in the jungle city of Thek. The approach used earlier didn't work this time.

Also, the Queen's first encounter with Alexander is not believable, even by Dunsany's rules. She finds him weeping over the death of his friend and immediately takes him in her lap and comforts him, as a mother would a small child with a skinned knee. This is simply ridiculous. The Queen is herself a haughty conqueror, and she is meeting the greatest conqueror of them all. She had originally come to challenge him to a battle.

The play turned out to be a disaster for Dunsany, but not for any of the above reasons. The problem was that Alexander dies in the *third* act, and the action continues for a good while afterwards. This was done on purpose, to show that the world goes on as usual after the death of a great man; but it brought objections from the noted actor-manager Martin Harvey, who was supposed to put the play on. He intended the leading role for himself and wanted to be the center of attention, with the curtain coming down immediately upon his demise. This Dunsany would not allow. When no compromise could be reached, he withdrew the play. It was published in 1926, but not performed until the Malvern Festival in 1938. The reception at Malvern was good, but *Alexander* went no further.

[55]

PATHWAYS TO ELFLAND

After such a long wait and so much effort, Dunsany must have been sorely disappointed. The play certainly brought him very little fame or money.

He had only one more play from his early period produced before the outbreak of the First World War. This was *The Queen's Enemies*, based on an incident recorded by Herodotus. A queen of Egypt invites all her enemies to a banquet in a crypt beneath the Nile, then lets the water in and drowns them. Her reason for doing so is simply that she could not bear the thought of having enemies. It disturbed her sleep.

A three-act play, *The Ginger Cat*, was scheduled for 1914, but cancelled because of the war, and never published or produced thereafter. The hostilities made as much of a mess of Dunsany's playwrighting career as it did the rest of his creative activities. The division, pre-war and post-war, is as clear as in his short stories.

It was his pre-war drama which brought him most of his theatrical reputation. *The Glittering Gate, King Argimenes, The Gods of the Mountain, The Golden Doom,* and *The Lost Silk Hat* were collected as *Five Plays* in 1914. All of them ran simultaneously on Broadway in 1916. England may have been grimly preoccupied, but America was still at peace and had time for the arts. As a result, Dunsany's reputation continued to build in the United States, while failing to do so at home. Americans, also, had no traditional prejudice against the writings of lords.

Five Plays and *Plays of Gods and Men* ultimately became his most widely circulated books. They were standard texts in schools.

It was in America that the first book about Dunsany was

" 'There's plenty of hope there, isn't there?' "
   . . . *The Glittering Gate*

[58]

produced, *Dunsany The Dramatist* by Edward Hale Bierstadt, published by Little, Brown, and Company in 1917. Normally, critical works are the province of university presses. Few non-academics read them. It is further testimony of how popular Dunsany had become that a commercial publisher attempted to cash in on him with secondary material.

Bierstadt was able to discuss the contents of *Five Plays*, plus *The Tents of the Arabs*, *A Night at an Inn*, and *The Queen's Enemies*, which were also being performed widely at the time. He mentions regretfully that he knows of the existence of *Alexander* and *The Laughter of the Gods*, but has been unable to read them since they have not yet (as of 1917) been published.

This period, roughly 1915-17, in America, was probably the high point of Dunsany's career as a dramatist. He never did quite so well again.

For the first two and a half years of the war, he wrote nothing except a few poems; but, after being wounded in the Easter Rebellion of 1916, coming down with tonsillitis, and later getting a desk job in England, he was able to turn out three one-act plays in the spring of 1917.

This was the darkest time of the war. Both sides had been stalemated for over two years, and men were dying in record numbers as the armies ground against one another uselessly. No end was in sight. The United States was still neutral. It seemed to Dunsany that the whole world was lost; and in his despair he wrote *The Old King's Tale*, about a king who is thwarted in his every attempt to return to his kingdom. Finally, when a herald comes seeking him, he does not reveal his identity, sure that the gods are

PATHWAYS TO ELFLAND

against him and he will never get back home. He relates
his woes to a pair of lovers whose marriage has been opposed by an oracle, and he tells them that there is hope
only for the future. The lovers should fight on, even if the
older generation is lost:

KING HODIATHON (to ARANIA)
No, no. It would be useless. The gods are against
me . . . Fight them! Fight the gods! They cannot stand
against youth!
(*Alexander and Three Small Plays*, p. 156)

Mark Amory calls this Dunsany's only autobiographical
play, and he is probably right. The beautiful, unrecover-
able land the king has lost can be seen as Dunsany's peaceful and relatively contented existence before the war. The
zenith of the British Empire and the Edwardian literary
scene had passed away; but the war was being fought,
Dunsany believed, so the next generation could have a
better life. He was only 39 at this time, but in his bleakest
moments he thought of himself as an old man whose day
was long gone.

As a personal statement, *The Old King's Tale* may have
meant something, but as drama it is very slight. There is
no on-stage conflict and no action. The king does nothing
except enter and tell of his life, and the lovers do nothing
but listen. The play would have been better as a short story,
and in fact it is a sort of short story, recited by the king,
with the rest being apparatus.

The second play of 1917 was a lot better. *Cheezo* is about
a curate who wants to marry a businessman's daughter,

but can't because the father disapproves. The problem is that the curate shows little potential for advancement in the church, having quarrelled with his bishop over the doctrine of eternal punishment. The businessman suggests he give in and get a promotion, but the curate won't compromise his ideals. Suddenly word is brought that the artificial cheese the businessman has been pushing has killed some test mice. He has too much of an investment at stake to pull out now, and as a matter of ego refuses to admit failure. He'll sell the stuff anyway, saying, "We'll advertise it and they'll eat it."

Faced with this perfidy, the curate proclaims, "I think I *do* believe in eternal punishment." He gets the girl, but isn't happy, having been forced to give up his cherished belief in the infinite mercy of God.

Advertising and artificial products were Dunsany's pet hates, but normally he didn't bring such sordid things into his art, preferring to write about the eternal and beautiful. In this case he made an exception, and in the introduction to *Plays of Near and Far* (1922) he explained:

> *Cheezo* tells of one of those rare occasions when it is permissible for an artist, and may be a duty, to leave his wider art in order to attack a definite evil. And the invention of "great new foods" is often a huge evil.
>
> *Cheezo* is a play of Right and Wrong, and Wrong triumphs. Were not this particular wrong triumphing at this particular date I should not have thought it a duty to attack it, and were it easily defeated it would not have been worth attacking.
>
> (p. v)

PATHWAYS TO ELFLAND

He defined allegory as "a dig at something local and limited . . . while appearing to tell of things on some higher plane," and insisted that he didn't write allegories, putting no hidden meanings in his plays. Indeed, the meaning of *Cheezo* is not hidden; and it is presented with some wit; but incisive satire it was not. The business world never noticed.

Next came *Fame and the Poet*, about a long-struggling poet who is finally visited by Fame, personified as a Greek goddess, only to find she talks like a Cockney street girl with dropped 'aitches, is loud, and has hopelessly bad manners. This is a reasonably good joke, but hardly enough to sustain a play. The obvious message is that fame is cheap and vulgar, not at all to be desired by the true artist. Considering that Dunsany's theatrical reputation in England was evaporating even as he wrote (he called the situation "black neglect"), this may be interpreted as sour grapes.

Immediately after the armistice, he tried to get back to normal with a three-act play, *The Old Folk of the Centuries*, which seems to have been his first attempt at children's theatre. The main character is a little boy who runs away from an urban workhouse and sees the country for the first time. He picks an apple in the orchard of a witch, is changed into a butterfly by her, then changed back by a kindly scientist, who sends him off to boarding school. But the school turns out to be such a horror—as only old-fashioned British boarding schools could be—that the boy runs away with a little girl, tricks the witch into making them both butterflies, and lives happily ever after.

The tone of the play is quite juvenile. It teeters on the edge between cute and cutesy. The children are invariably

PLAYS

nice, the adults distorted according to the way a child would see each of them. Sir Joseph Wundle, the entomologist, is kindly and seems to know everything, while the sole delight of the boarding school master seems to be asking his students impossible questions and caning them at the slightest excuse. If the reader takes the viewpoint of a child, the play can be quite enjoyable. There is a real feeling of relief when the boy gains the freedom of a butterfly at the end. Children would doubtless be cheering at this point.

The Old Folk of the Centuries does not seem to have been successful. If it was ever performed at all, it wasn't done widely. The reading public saw little of it, since its only printing was a 900-copy edition in 1930.

Another juvenile play, also from 1918, may have fared even worse. *The Prince of Stamboul* (one act) is sufficiently obscure that Amory does not mention it, and the title does not appear in the British Museum catalogue. The most readily available early publication (that is, dating from Dunsany's lifetime; it is included in *The Ghosts of the Heaviside Layer*) is in a textbook, *Short Plays for Junior and Senior Highschools*, edited by James Plaisted Webber and Hanson Hart Webster, published by Houghton Mifflin in 1925. This credits *Harper's Bazaar* in the acknowledgements. The title appears in the "books by" listings in some editions of Dunsany's works from the 1930s, without telling what it is. It is no longer listed by the 1940s, as if Dunsany would rather have forgotten it.

The Prince of Stamboul is a very minor play, which starts nowhere and stays there. A sick girl will die if she doesn't get some sleep, but she can't sleep until a playmate plays

[63]

PATHWAYS TO ELFLAND

"Home Sweet Home" on his penny flute. Unfortunately he lives too far away, but by a happy coincidence one of the world's great musicians, the Prince of the title, is passing through town. He plays for the child, superbly, but this won't do, so he sends his car to fetch the boy, who plays badly and puts the girl to sleep. The end. Charitably, this might be called a sentimental trifle, but few are likely to be charitable after reading it. One is reminded of the Oscar Wilde quote on Dickens, "A man would have to be utterly without a heart to read about the death of Little Nell without laughing."

Children's theatre was not Dunsany's forté, it seems.

He did, however, have one more big success. This was *If*, a four-act play written in 1919 and performed in England in 1921. It was his single greatest triumph in terms of the number of performances and money made, nothing short of a smash hit which ran for hundreds of nights. When it came to New York in 1927, it also went over well, even if the *New York Times* critic called it "slight."

The charge was actually justified. *If*, for all its length, has no more substance to it than many of the one-acters. There is a decidedly watered-down quality to it. The plot involves a respectable English suburbanite who uses a magic crystal to go back in time and set right anything he chooses. Like Wells's miracle-worker, he thinks small, and catches a train he once missed, despite his wife's fears that this will change their whole lives, even to the point that the two of them never met in the new past which is created. Dunsany was trifling with time-travel/alternate-universe concepts which later generations of science-fiction writers explored in depth, but all he did was trifle. He was using the idea as a gimmick to produce an amusing comedy and nothing more.

Sure enough, the wife is correct, for not long after our hero catches the train he meets a lady who is owed a fortune by a sheik in the East; and he is so taken with her plight that he goes to Shaldomir, a land on the far side of Persia, to collect the debt. The usual run of exotic adventures result. The Englishman becomes king, but is betrayed, and ends up back in London penniless. The spell of the crystal compels him to return to his house on the same night he left, only now it isn't his house. In the new time-stream his wife has married someone else. Fortunately, when the crystal is broken everything is set right.

The play contains some inventive scenes and witty lines, and it must, in its way, be considered a pioneering time-travel story, but it has serious weaknesses. The "eastern" setting becomes transparently fake when we have enough time to get used to it. Dunsany was still not developing his characters, and this time he didn't have Greek classicism, gods, and fate as an excuse. The play is simply over-extended fluff. It may have gone over well because audiences *like* fluff now and then, but the problem with such a play is that it may raise a chuckle or two, and then the audience goes on to something *else* which raises a chuckle or two just as readily. It has no staying power, as indeed *If* didn't.

From this point on, Dunsany's career as a playwright went downhill very rapidly. He was never able to follow up *If*, and nothing ruins a writer faster than being on the verge of becoming a major talent and failing to do so. Predictably, Dunsany went into the stage where critics pronounced him a has-been and vastly over-rated. Worse, his writing began to suffer.

It was to become a familiar pattern. In every phase of his work, he would begin very well and get better, producing his best work of any particular type very early. Then he would remain at a certain level for a while and start to decline. After his early successes, he seldom made significant advances and tended to remain satisfied with what he was doing. Then, as inspiration ran dry and repetition set in, the material would become increasingly trivial.

Of course he didn't know that he was finished after *If*. He thought he had hit the big-time. He tried to follow up his success at once, but the attempt fizzled.

He began a three-act play in October of 1922, set it aside for a while, and finished it in a few days in April 1923. This was *Lord Adrian*, and it turned out to be one of those works in which the whole is not as great as the sum of the parts. It actually contains some of his best writing and his most vividly depicted characters, but the hiatus between the beginning and the completion of the play may have taken its toll. The pieces don't fit together and the ending seems tacked on.

Lord Sandborough, the grandson of the iron-willed Duke of Fenland and Arden, is engaged to marry the Duke's secretary, Bessie. The two are incompatible, unfortunately; and by mutual consent they break off the engagement. Furious, the Duke tries to disinherit his grandson; but is thwarted because the will of an earlier duke clearly states that the family property must be left to a direct descendant. There are only two, Sandborough and his father, the Duke's son, from whom Sandborough will inherit. The frustrated Duke dodges this in a novel manner by having himself injected with the extract of an ape gland. This rejuvenates him until he no longer seems 80, but a mere 50. Then *he* marries the girl and sires a son, Lord Adrian, who is to inherit.

So far we have a superlatively written social comedy with science-fictional touches. The conflict between the Duke and his grandson is clearly set up, and the plot proceeds with his attempt to bypass Sandborough in favor of Adrian. But then, almost as if Dunsany had changed his mind about what he was doing, the play turns into something else.

Adrian finds that he has a greater affinity toward animals than mankind, presumably as a result of his simian origins. He resents the way men have exploited and slaughtered other creatures, and plots to lead the animals in revolt against mankind. Humanity's technological superiority, he believes, is due to the chance discovery of fire, so to set things even he starts to teach the badgers and foxes to make fire with flints. In the end, when something seems about to happen, Adrian is shot by the Duke's gamekeeper, more aborting the play than concluding it.

The reason that the pieces fail to come together is that *both* plays, the social comedy about the Duke and his grandson, and the story of the revolt of the animals, are aborted rather than worked to their conclusions. Imagine Shaw's *Man and Superman* invaded in the middle by a misanthropic Tarzan who is conveniently run over by a truck at the end and you'll get the idea.

Trouble arose when the play was being produced. The director wanted large-scale changes and Dunsany protested. But he had learned a little with *Alexander*, and a

[67]

compromise was reached. *Adrian* was performed in Hull in 1923, but disputes arose again, and it never got to London or New York. When it was done in Dublin in 1937, the *New York Times* reviewer said it seemed more the work of a beginner than an experienced playwright. Another sign of Dunsany's declining fortunes was the fact that the play was not published by his regular publisher (Putnam) but by a small press in a 300-copy edition in 1933.

A final full-length play followed, *Mr. Faithful*, a comedy. It is more satisfactory than *Lord Adrian*, if less inventive in content, and wittier than *If*, so it must be rated as one of Dunsany's best longer plays. It is a canine play, although written in 1922, a full decade before he came to what Amory calls his "Great Canine Period" in prose. The story is about a former World-War-I army officer who literally leads a dog's life in order to marry the girl he loves. Like most ex-officers, he can't find a job, and his fiance's father won't give consent unless he can hold some position for six months. So, when he sees an advertisement offering 50 pounds for a watchdog, he takes the money and serves all the functions of a dog, chasing cats up trees, barking at callers, sleeping outside in a barrel, and so on. His intent is to do his job "properly," i.e. as dogs have always done it. This leads to trouble when the future father-in-law, a true Dunsanian businessman with an urge to fleece everyone he meets, tries to swindle the gullible employer. Mr. Faithful protects his master's property by biting the scoundrel on the leg. Ultimately the father has our hero kidnapped so he can't finish the last few days of the allotted time, but the daughter calls the police and reports a dog theft. When a policeman arrives, he gets a quick idea of what is going on and leaves to summon the men in the white suits. As with *Lord Adrian*, the play just ends rather than resolving. A great deal of potentially funny material about the suitor's legal status as a dog is wasted.

Mr. Faithful was performed in London, but without much success, and it never got to New York. It was finally published by Samuel French as an acting edition in 1935, so it probably enjoyed scattered exposure on amateur stages for a while before dropping out of sight. Chances are it would do well if revived today in college theatres. The audiences could sympathise with the unemployment problem, and the wit of the play hasn't dated any.

Many short plays were written during the twenties, and the bulk of them were published in three books, *Plays of Near and Far* (1922), *Seven Modern Comedies* (1938) and *Plays for Earth and Air* (1937). Two more, along with *The Old King's Tale*, fill out *Alexander and Three Small Plays* (1925). These short plays range in quality from fairly good to utterly trivial, without varying much in actual technique. In all, most of the plot is carried through dialogue. In the best, the plot is worth bothering with. In the worst, it isn't.

Among the best are *His Sainted Grandmother*, in which a modern "liberated" girl gets shockingly candid advice on romancing from the ghost of an allegedly proper Victorian matron; *The Amusements of Khan Karuda*, about an Eastern mystic whose powers are dramatically demonstrated when he turns a batch of rudely skeptical British diners into animals; and *The Evil Kettle*, which shows how James Watt's inspiration to build the steam engine and industrialise (and uglify) England came from the Devil. The worst make one wonder why they were ever written, let alone performed or published. For example, *A Matter of Honor* is just a scene in which a dying man, who has won a bet, calls his friends to him and forgives them their debt. Apparently Dunsany thought the irony was enough to carry.

Some of the short plays are vehicles for jokes. *The Hopeless Passion of Mr. Bunyon* is about a clerk who is fired from a store because he spends so much time staring at a mannekin. He begs to be allowed to stay, even without pay. The boss refuses. At the last minute the mannekin moves, and is discovered to be a real girl who was hired to stand perfectly still in the window all this time, without the knowledge of the manager, apparently. This may not make any sense, but it does provoke a slight one-time laugh.

Fame Comes Late is a variation of *Fame and the Poet*. This time Fame shows up only after the poet has struggled for many years, and she is middle-aged and worn out, with her sandals soggy from the rain. An amusing conceit, but very little is done with it.

The Pumpkin contains some interesting ideas, even if they're half-developed. The play derives from a remark made by Dunsany's friend, the noted scientist William Beebe. Upon hearing someone discuss the possibilities of atomic energy, Beebe said, "Now we know what the novas are—people like you monkeying with the atom." A farmer sells a prize pumpkin to a scientist for an exorbitant price, then wonders why the scientist wanted it so badly. Rumors fly, and before long the local people are convinced that the scientist intends to start a nuclear fission reaction with the pumpkin, which will spread to all matter on Earth, blowing up the world. Before much happens, however, the misunderstanding is resolved; and the play ends just as it

[70]

is starting to get interesting.

At the very end of his dramatic career (middle 1930s), Dunsany began to write scripts for the radio. This medium is ideally suited for fantasy, since the audience can be made to imagine things which would be difficult to produce on stage or screen. Had Dunsany put a little effort into it, he might have made some genuine advances in radio drama, but he didn't. He was still coasting, his work descreasing in interest.

The Use of Man made adequate use of the possibilities of radio in its account of a fox hunter who thinks all animals not useful to man should be exterminated. In a dream he is brought before a tribunal of animals, who try to figure out what good man is to any other species. The sycophantic dog says man is important "because he is man," but aside from that the only advocate the hunter can find is the mosquito, who finds man a source of food. Had he not come up with two, mankind would have been destroyed.

Rather obviously this play would not have worked on the stage. Either there would have been only one actor with a lot of offstage voices, or actors would have to wear animal costumes. Either way would have looked silly.

The Seventh Symphony has the spirits of the immortals, Beethoven, Milton, Herrick, Cervantes, Shelley, etc., driven from the dreams of a dying composer when the landlady inadvertently changes the channel on the radio from classical music to jazz. "Good" art is driven away by "bad," literally.

In other plays, Dunsany was less at ease with the radio format. He never came to terms with the audience's inability to see the scene and characters. To make up for this,

PATHWAYS TO ELFLAND

he would have his characters describe everything, as if to a blind person, rather than drop enough hints to let the imagination fill in the rest. The result was unbelievable dialogue. The worst excesses occur in two adaptations of pre-war stories, *The Bureau de Change* ("The Bureau d'Echange De Mauz" from *The Last Book of Wonder*) and *The Golden Dragon Cuty* ("The Wonderful Window" from *The Book of Wonder*), which are little more than second-hand descriptions of things happening elsewhere. "The Wonderful Window" is simply not suited for the radio, since it depends so heavily on what the protagonist *sees*. Both plays read terribly and would probably play worse on the air. To change them into radio plays, Dunsany seems to have merely carved the stories up into dialogue, then added characters to say "Oh, look at that," as an excuse for describing something.

All the plays of the post-war period suffer from a lack of intensity, perhaps from a lack of commitment on the part of the author. They fail to do what they set out to do because they don't do it enough. They may make political statements (*In Holy Russia*, about a peasant's vision of the famine and suffering the revolution will bring), satirize the theatre itself (*The Journey of the Soul*, in which actors, directors, producers, etc. foul up great drama), or present melodramatic plots (*Atmospherics*, about a man trapped in a train compartment with an escaped lunatic), but they are never incisive, particularly convincing, moving, or ultimately memorable.

After *Plays for Earth and Air*, Dunsany's days as a dramatist were over. Two more plays were apparently performed, but never published. *The Strange Lover*, which premiered in Dublin in 1938, was science fiction, about an artificial man. *The Road* was, according to Hazel Littlefield Smith's *Lord Dunsany: King of Dreams*, written for the Shoreham Players in the early 1950s. Presumably it was performed by them. A third play, *Power*, was never finished. Dunsany worked on it for a while about 1954.

How do we account for the decline and collapse of Dunsany's career as a playwright? Sheer lack of quality is the most obvious answer. Since many of his later plays were not nearly as good as his earlier ones, producers became less willing to put them on and audiences less eager to see them. But why did some of his best plays, or at least fairly presentable plays, like *Lord Adrian* and *Mr. Faithful*, fail to get anywhere? Why were his good ones allowed to go into obscurity?

Trends should be considered. The romantic school of writing in general, and fantasy in particular, were dealt a severe blow by the Depression. Fantasy novelists, such as James Branch Cabell, who were best-sellers in the 1920s, were barely able to get published in the later '30s. Fantasy short fiction retreated into the pulp magazines. In theatre, the realistic fashion took over, and where it gave way to absurdism it was still far away from the sort of fantasy Dunsany was doing. A producer who deifies Eugene O'Neill and Arthur Miller or Samuel Beckett and Eugene Ionesco is going to have no room for Dunsany.

So it has been ever since. In the '30s the idea arose that respectable literature had to be realistic. Anything imaginative was suspect. This sort of thinking is still entrenched in university English departments. Since live stage cannot attract a large audience because of the sheer logistics, it tends to be dominated by cliques of critics or academics, and thus is far more conservative than most areas of the arts.

Once a type of writing has been out of fashion for more than a generation, it has to be rediscovered. Supernatural fantasy on the stage, the sort of thing that Dunsany did best, would be difficult for a producer to attempt. A successful play of the type might make others easier, but that first one would run the risk of complete incomprehension. Barring that, it might delight audiences the same way *The Lord of the Rings* delighted a reading public which had never seen a fantasy novel before.

Dunsany's social comedies are less victims of changing fashion. The best plays of Shaw, Wilde, and the rest are still being performed. A play like *Mr. Faithful* is the same kind of thing, only not as good. It was old-fashioned by the time it was written, certainly, but that alone shouldn't have been enough to destroy its chances. Christopher Fry's *The Lady's Not For Burning* is an Elizabethan verse play written in 1949. It happens to be a very *good* one, and it is still doing very well. Since there has always been an audience for Elizabethan verse plays, Fry had one foot in the door; and that was all he needed. Had Dunsany written a genuinely superior Edwardian drawing-room comedy in the '30s or at any time, he should have been able to do the same.

By the 1930s, Dunsany seems to have not been trying very hard. As a result, his plays got worse and went nowhere. So he didn't think it worthwhile to put much effort into them. At the same time, he was writing some of his best novels and the Jorkens series had given him a second wind as a short story writer. Plays had become a minor part of his output, and he abandoned them completely when the public ceased to be interested.

He also had a problem common to writers who don't have to make a living off their work: he didn't push his plays hard enough. A writer has to ignore rejections and send a manuscript out again and again until it sells. When one of Dunsany's plays was turned down a couple of times, he'd just let it sit, as he did with *Alexander*, or, to a more extreme degree, *The Ginger Cat*.

There is a particularly revealing passage in *While the Sirens Slept*:

> I always looked on the job of offering plays, or books, to managers or publishers, and touting them successfully, as being work that might occupy a lifetime if done thoroughly, and I decided long ago that one could not do two things, write one's best work, and go around explaining to people that it was good, or trying to make them believe so. Therefore when I have written a play or a book and had it typed, and offered to one or two people, I go on to write another book, which I should not have the leisure to do if I spent all my time on the fortunes of the other. These fortunes are really not the writer's concern: the staging and acting of a play are other men's jobs, and a man can only do his own.
>
> (p. 18)

Maybe what Dunsany needed was a good agent.

[75]

Novels

By the early 1920s Dunsany had become dissatisfied with the meagre recognition he was receiving for his short stories, and perhaps he had already sensed that his involvement in the theatre wouldn't last. So he turned to novels, hoping to do better.

In doing so, he encountered the usual problems of a short story writer trying to write novels. It took him a while to learn that a novel is not a short story only made longer.

A case in point is his first, *The Chronicles of Rodriguez* (1922), which suffers for want of any overall plot structure. It is little more than a chain of separate events strung together on the slightest excuse. But, as might be expected from Dunsany, it has its strengths.

The *Chronicles* introduce the typical protagonist of Dunsany's novels, the naïve young man who knows very little about the real world but has a head full of romantic notions. Just as typically, the world fails to meet his expectations at first, but ultimately events somehow manage to fall into place so that he isn't too disappointed.

Our hero is a Spaniard, Don Rodriguez, "son of the

Lord of the Valleys of Argento Harez, whose heights see not Valladolid," who is bequeathed a sword and a mandolin by his dying father and commanded to seek glory, romance, and adventure. His brother, a bit of a dullard, gets the family estates. In the space of twelve chapters, Rodriguez manages to acquire a castle, a beautiful wife, and a Sancho Panza-like sidekick. He even rights a few wrongs, as a noble knight of romance should, even though sometimes he succeeds through sheer luck or the incompetence of his opponents.

The story is Dunsany's version of *Don Quixote*, save that Dunsany has neither the heart nor the inclination to burlesque romantic fiction with the ferocity of Cervantes. He is fully aware that life isn't the way Rodriguez thinks it is, but seems to be gently saying, "well, wouldn't it be nice?" As a result, things end happily, even if the author must result to blatant string-pulling to make them do so. When our hero has captured a knight who turns out to be a fake and thus has no castle with which to ransom himself, rather than leave Rodriguez forlorn, Dunsany brings in a bunch of outlaws, who seem to be strays from the Robin Hood cycle, to build him a castle at the last minute. Thus, when all possibilities have been exhausted and dreams seem dashed, all is set right, just for sentimental reasons. It may very well be the whole point of the book that a *deus ex machina* is required.

Some of the individual episodes are very good. There is a visit to a sinister inn where one pulls a rope for the doorbell and hears a scream, the rope being attached to a hook embedded in some unfortunate. After putting an end to the host's poor hospitality, Rodriguez and his companion come upon a professor of magic, who sends their spirits to the surface of the sun in a stunning burst of imagery. The magician's house is fascinating. Unfortunately the whole sequence has nothing whatever to do with the overall story.

Many of the episodes could almost stand as short stories, which suggests that Dunsany was not completely at ease with the idea of writing a novel. He remarked that he preferred short stories:

> . . . it appears to me that in a page of a short story there must be more art than in a page of a novel, just as in a square inch of an ivory carving there is more art than in a square inch of a wall of a palace: everything in fact in a short story may be fairly intense, as in a play, whereas there is room for a certain amount of rambling in a novel.
>
> (*While the Sirens Slept*, p. 38)

The trouble, then, is in Dunsany's conception of what a novel is. A novel also needs compactness. Its greater length demands that there be more substance than there is in a short story, not that the same amount be spread out thin. Dunsany later stated that he saw novels as being about 70,000 words long. Obviously he wrote to that length, then stopped, without paying much heed to the internal needs of the material at hand. Content should dictate length, not the other way around. Even writing that is as beautiful as Dunsany's can tire the reader after a while. This book would have benefitted from judicious trimming.

The same is true of his second novel, *The King of Elfland's*

Daughter (1924), which is still his most famous. It would have been a masterpiece at half the length. More unified than *Rodriguez*, it still bogs down in an excess of the inconsequential.

One very definite advance in *Daughter* is an ability to make the best of the thematic material. *Don Rodriguez* only occasionally touches on what it is actually about, without exploring the differences between romantic preconceptions and the real world in any depth. But in his second novel, Dunsany produced a full treatment of his major subject, The Loss of Elfland.

First, what does he mean by "Elfland"? It is more than just a country inhabited by elves. It is a timeless realm beyond "the frontier of twilight." One can see that frontier in the east sometimes in the glow of dawn, or more often in the deepening shadows of evening. Elfland is filled with unearthly beauty, "which may only be told of in song," all created out of the mind of the Elfking, who is thus more a god than a monarch, and on whose mental calm the peace of his domain depends. At one point the place is compared to a deep, dim pool, in which fishes lie still. A disturbance sends ripples throughout all the land.

Elfland is both a place and a state of existence. It doesn't conform to mundane rules of geography or anything else. If the King chooses, he can withdraw it so far from mortal lands that the intervening stretch "would weary a comet," and then let it flow back like "the tide over flat sand."

It is also a literalized, multiplex metaphor for the imagination, for the lost innocence of childhood, for everything which lies beyond our grasp. At one point Alveric, the hero, while wandering through the wasteland left after the

[79]

PATHWAYS TO ELFLAND

King has pulled his borders back far from Earth, finds an old toy which had been broken and discarded many years before. He also hears faint bits of old songs lingering in the air. When he grows older and settles down with an ordinary wife and thinks only of making a living, he ceases to dream and thus loses the vision of Elfland. He can no longer see the Elfin Mountains when he looks eastward at dawn or sunset. All that is for youth, he says.

Since most of Dunsany's novels following this one deal with the progressive loss of this vision, obviously the idea meant something to him. An autobiographical interpretation is certainly possible. He was forty-six when he wrote *The King of Elfland's Daughter*, which is not exactly young. The war was between him and that first, exuberantly imaginative phase of his career. His enchanted dreams were slipping away; but, brilliantly, rather than write weaker and weaker stories, he turned this very loss into his subject matter.

In *The King of Elfland's Daughter*, dreams ultimately triumph. Alveric, prince of the earthly kingdom of Erl, is sent into Elfland to make off with the lady of the title. Unfortunately, once he marries her, he succumbs to conventional and unromantic views, insisting that Lirazel, the Elvish princess, become a proper Christian and cease worshipping stars, flowers, etc. She conforms for a while, bears him a son, but is unhappy. Meanwhile, her father has written a powerful rune on a parchment, which he sends to her. When she reads it, she loses touch with all mundane things and blows away with the autumn leaves, back into Elfland. For years Alveric searches, but the lost love cannot be regained, literally because the King has withdrawn his borders, metaphorically because Alveric has grown older and duller. He travels about with a company of lunatics, who actually hold him back for fear that Elfland would drown all their own fancies. All seems hopeless, but Lirazel misses Alveric, and persuades her father to use his last great rune, which causes Elfland to flow over Erl, enchanting everything and closing it off from time, except for a small space around a chapel where a friar and several stodgy citizens, who can't approve of pagan things, may live out their last days. Dunsany always portrayed clergymen favorably in his novels, so he dealt with the friar gently. Besides, some readers doubtless found it shocking that paganism and magic win out. Again, the story is a dream of the impossible. Dunsany knows there is no such thing as Elfland, but is once more saying, "Wouldn't it be nice?"

In conception the novel is certainly magnificent, but there are just too many unicorn-hunting scenes, and quite a few more nature descriptions than any but the most patient reader can stand. Some of these are beautiful, but they pale from repetition.

The prose is often very deft, as might be expected. We are told of a witch who lives in a cottage "on the high land, near the thunder, which used to roll in summer among the hills," and there are many other examples of descriptions which are both imaginative and precise. The previously mentioned "space which would weary a comet" is excellent. Other writers might have taken paragraphs to convey the same sense of infinite waste.

But there are times when the language becomes affected and precious. Dunsany described it as "as close to poetry" as he ever got, which was not a good thing coming from him, since his poetry was the least impressive area of his writing. Sometimes he is a trifle too vague to be effective:

> And the wild things that Earth has guessed at and the things hidden even from legend were moved to sing age-old songs that their memories had forgotten. And fabulous things of the air were lured down out of great heights. And emotions unknown and unthought of troubled the calm of Elfland.
>
> (pp. 217–18)

In other words: I'm going to tell you about something so amazing, so beautiful, that earthly concepts don't apply, something beyond your wildest dreams and imaginings, of which no ancient bard ever sang, something you never read about . . . and so on for a page or two, all of which promises a great deal and delivers nothing. The above passage contains nothing concrete or visual. We cannot hear "age-old songs," nor can we see the "fabulous things of the air" without more information. We are merely told they are age-old and fabulous, and are expected to take Dunsany's word for it. This kind of writing is simply not as adept as that of "The Fortress Unvanquishable" or many of the other early short stories, which promise wonders and then produce them while remaining masterpieces of compression. At its worst, the prose of *Daughter* is murky and bloated.

Occasionally, as strange as it may seem for Dunsany, there are even clumsy constructions. Perhaps the attempt to be self-consciously poetical is at fault. "Talking through

[82]

his nose," to borrow a phrase from the late James Blish, he strives for archaicism and inversion, and gives us this:

> . . . there was Guhic, who had first thought of it, after speaking with his wife, an upland farmer of clover pastures near Erl . . .
>
> (p. 37)

Guhic married a lady farmer of the uplands? More likely what Dunsany meant was, "There was Guhic, an upland farmer of clover pastures near Erl, who had first thought of it, after speaking with his wife."

Still, much of the novel shows Dunsany in top form. The style is a lot better in places where he isn't rambling, where some imaginative concept is being presented or something is happening. The first ninety pages or so, the fruitless search of Alveric, and the final coming of Elfland into Erl are brilliant sequences. It is on the strength of these, no doubt, that the novel has endured, when others which are actually better put together are out of print and forgotten.

Two years later came *The Charwoman's Shadow*, which showed another significant advance in novelistic technique. *The King of Elfland's Daughter* surpassed *Don Rodriguez* in that it had a coherent plot under all the padding. *The Charwoman's Shadow* went a step further by dispensing with the padding. It was the first Dunsany novel to really *be* a novel, rather than merely a prose narrative stretched to 70,000 words by any means available.

It is marginally a sequel to *Don Rodriguez*. The setting is the same imaginary "Golden Age" of Spain, only several generations later. A descendant of one of the characters in the earlier book plays a minor role. The blithe mutilation of the Spanish language continues; this time the hero's name is Ramon Alonzo Matthew-Mark-Luke-John of the Tower and Rocky Forest.

Ramon is sent by his father to learn magic at the house of a magician. There he is tricked out of his shadow (which the magician cuts off at the heels with a special knife), only to find that without it he is an outcast from the rest of mankind. Everybody knows that someone without a shadow is tainted by the black arts. In one scene Ramon is sitting among ordinary folk, and the sun goes down. Their shadows lengthen; but his, being an imitation given him by the magician, *doesn't*.

In the magician's house he meets an old charwoman, whose shadow has similarly been stolen. When he recovers it, her youth is restored.

The writing in *Shadow* is an improvement over that in *The King of Elfland's Daughter*. When Dunsany describes something, he makes it real. Beautiful things are beautiful. The mysterious is mysterious, but underneath the mystery there is more than a pile of adjectives. The prose is less flowery and there is more dialogue.

The strengths of the book are very great. The magician, his practice, and his dwelling are all presented in a wealth of detail, resulting in one of the most delightful treatments of magic in all literature. The old fellow is as much of a villain as the book has, but there are sympathetic glimpses of him as a confused fumbler who can't find things in his laboratory under all the stuffed crocodiles. He is a whimsical and yet human creation, who surely has descendants in the works of later writers like T.H. White and John

[84]

Bellairs. Anemone, the charwoman, is believable in her age and her plight and also in her restored youth. This too is an admirable accomplishment, since restored maidens tend to turn cardboard in most fantasy novels. The only serious problem is that Ramon Alonzo is too much of a typical Naïve Young Man and never quite a three-dimensional character. He is a good two-dimensional imitation who behaves like a human being, but lacks emotional depth. He is certainly serviceable while the other characters, the beautiful writing, and the endlessly inventive plot maintain the reader's interest; but he is no more than that.

Happily, there are no long hunting scenes or other irrelevant episodes. The book is certainly Dunsany's best pure fantasy novel, and his second best all told, surpassed only by *The Curse of the Wise Woman*, about which more later.

Thematically, *The Charwoman's Shadow* is part of the progression away from the vision of Elfland. The book is still brimming with magic, and pagan things are treated sympathetically when in conflict with the (equally sympathetic) Christian clergy, but magic does not flow over the Earth this time. It withdraws. In order to escape damnation, the magician flees to the Land Beyond the Moon's Rising, whence he and all the followers of the Old Way can never return. Bereft of enchantment, the Golden Age of Spain ends.

Magic also keeps its distance in *The Blessing of Pan* (1928), but so does, unfortunately, much of Dunsany's storytelling ability. While there is more and better handled dialogue in this book, and (for the first time in a Dunsany novel) familiar lands are described effectively, it is not an advance

[85]

PATHWAYS TO ELFLAND

over its predecessor because in just as many ways it is inferior to *The Charwoman's Shadow*. The padding is back. In fact the novel is *mostly* padding. One suspects that its natural length is on the order of 20,000 words, a novella at best.

The plot has to do with mysterious and enchanting music which wafts down from the Kentish hills at evening, causing otherwise respectable people to want to go up there and join in wild revels. The protagonist, a timid, incompetent, but basically *nice* vicar, writes to his bishop, reporting an outbreak of paganism. The bishop insists he has been working too hard. Nothing is done. Ultimately paganism wins, and the vicar finds himself up in the hills offering sacrifice to Pan. The local source of miracles, the tomb of St. Ethelbruda, loses its power to cure warts.

The problem is that Dunsany takes much too long to reach this conclusion, and in the meantime he offers nothing wondrous, just more vague hints of beauties beyond the hills, like the previously quoted passage from *The King of Elfland's Daughter* only in plainer language. There is little that is concrete. Pan never makes an appearance to liven things up, even at the end. The plot is too simple, lacking complication. It may be logical that nothing is done, but it is difficult to tell an interesting story about nothing.

The previous novels had been met with basically good, if slightly patronizing, critical reception. The reviews of this one weren't as good, even from critics who weren't shocked at the ending. It isn't hard to see why.

It is therefore a bit of a surprise that his best-received novel, which many consider his finest, came next. However, there was a hiatus of several years, during which

Dunsany wrote many of the early Jorkens stories, contrib-
uted lots of bad verse to newspapers, and travelled through
India. Perhaps because it had a longer period of gestation,
The Curse of the Wise Woman is more substantial.

It was written, according to Lady Dunsany, in "three and
a half breathless months" in 1933, and published that year.
This time Dunsany showed a full command of style and
structure, and for the first time his characters came completely alive. For the first time he used Irish life as his
source material. Twenty years earlier Yeats had all but
kicked him out of the self-styled Irish Renaissance for failing to do so. Dunsany's reply then was that if someone
were to found a society for medieval Italian poets, they
obviously couldn't include Dante, who didn't write about
Italy, but a different place entirely. Now he produced a
full-fledged Irish novel to the astonishment of those who
said he couldn't do it.

Everything done wrong in *The King of Elfland's Daugher*
and *The Blessing of Pan* is here done properly. There are
long nature descriptions, and even a fox hunt which runs
for three chapters, but it all comes off splendidly, perhaps
because Dunsany was writing about something he knew
and appreciated. Thus, even when a scene did little to
advance the plot, he could make the wordage worthwhile
for its own sake. There is little which is vague or which
promises in vain. The Irish countryside (around Meath,
where Dunsany Castle is) comes across so vividly the reader
is all but transported there:

> . . . and for a while we walked in silence over the
> rushes. The moss lay grey all around us, crisp as a dry

PATHWAYS TO ELFLAND

sponge, while we stepped on the heather and the
rushes, the heather all covered with dead grey buds,
the rushes a pale sandy color. I had never walked the
bog in the Spring before, and was surprised at the
greyness of it. But some bright mosses remained, scar-
let and brilliant green; and all along the edge of the
bog under the hills lay a ribbon of gorse, and the fields
flashed bright above it, so that the bog lay like a dull
stone set in gold, with a row of emeralds around the
golden ring. A snipe got up brown, and turned, and
flashed white in turning. A curlew rose and sped away
down the sky with swift beats of his long wings and
loud outcry, giving the news, "Man, Man," to all whose
peace was endangered by our approach, and a skylark
shot up and sang, and stayed above us singing. The
pools that in the winter lay between the islands of the
heather, and that Martin used to tell me were bottom-
less, were most of them grey slime now, topped with
a crust that looked as if it almost might bear one.

(pp. 212–13)

Beyond this looms Tir-nan-Og, the Land of Youth of
Celtic lore. We never actually see it, and no one ever gets
there, unlike the villagers in *The Blessing of Pan*, who at
least reach the hills from which the music comes. Elfland
has retreated to the very periphery of the novel. There is
no outright fantasy element, save for the ambiguous curses
of a local witch that may or may not be responsible for
stopping the depredations of a peat company intent on
ruining the bog. But in any case, between the finest magical
cursing and conjuring scenes Dunsany ever wrote and the

[88]

"Such speed was new to the dog."
... *The King of Elfland's Daughter*

[90]

vision of Tir-nan-Og, the book has the feel of the purest
fantasy. There is also enough of a plot to keep it going,
involving the Troubles in Ireland, although apparently
shifted back to the time of Dunsany's youth in the late 19th
century; a lonely boy growing up by himself on an estate
by the bog; and the attempt to drive off the exploiters.
There is also a gamekeeper who thinks he has lost his soul
by yearning for Tir-nan-Og, and his plight is genuinely
touching. The characterization of the protagonist, who
tells the story in the first person, is very good. There are
some autobiographical elements, a rare thing for Dunsany.
   Critical acclaim seems to have bordered on the ecstatic,
and the readers liked the book well enough to have kept
it in print until the early 1950s. It is still in the "books by"
lists in Dunsany's last volumes. It was reprinted again in
1972. Probably its lack of greater staying power stems from
the fact that it is so unlike the sort of fantasy for which he
is best remembered, and also because it is so unlike his
other Irish novels. None of the others are nearly as good.
   Obviously the success of *Wise Woman* spurred Dunsany
on. There were three novels in 1936, *Rory and Bran*, *My
Talks With Dean Spanley*, and *Up In the Hills*.
   Rory and Bran is about Ireland again, with magic around
the edges, but this time the magic is clearly a delusion in
the mind of an allegedly 19-year-old youth who frequently
seems more like 12. This bookish lad, without a practical
thought in his head, is sent by his father to take cattle to
market. Like Jack of beanstalk fame, he is promptly hood-
winked out of them, but saved again and again by Bran,
who is obviously smarter. Bran is a dog. The main problem
with the book is that nowhere does Dunsany come out and

[91]

state this. He later claimed that it was perfectly obvious to him, so there was no need to explain, but one suspects deliberate ambiguity. Bran drinks out of puddles, but so does Rory, so that's hardly a clue. Whenever Bran utters a sound, the verb used is one which could denote either human or animal noises. Bran is never described as barking, wagging his tail, scratching his fleas, or doing anything else overtly canine. The result is a blindfold-the-reader story, wherein an essential fact is withheld which would be perfectly obvious if the reader were able to see the scene. Seeing the scene is very much what fiction is about. Storytelling is a visual art in the mind's eye. With a deliberate deception like this the reader gets to the end and discovers he hasn't really read the book, and now must go back and re-imagine it the way everything really happened. He has been lied to and cheated, as surely as the science-fiction reader who discovers at the end of the story that the hero is really a giant lobster and the invading monsters are Earthmen.

In *Rory and Bran* it is possible to read the whole book without catching on. Amory quotes one reviewer who remarked that the character "is rather quiet for an Irishman." This can only be distracting because the plot does not hinge on the fact that Bran is a dog. The best way to read the novel is forewarned.

Again the nature descriptions are very good and the atmosphere is maintained well. We see more of the Irish countryside than in *The Curse of the Wise Woman* because the hero must travel, and we meet more people as Rory and Bran wander hither and yon with a band of tinkers. (Tinkers are Irish gypsies, who, at least at the time, rode about in wagons and made meager livings repairing pots and doing odd jobs.) Significantly, Dunsany makes it abundantly obvious that there are no legendary heroes among the clouds atop the mountains, and that the supposedly prophetic talisman, the Stone of the Sea, is really a piece of ocean-smoothed glass. The vision of Elfland is fading fast.

Dunsany's thesis is that simple people are better off with their beliefs and better off kept in their place. An ardent Irish nationalist (then or now) might object that this is patronizing, but Dunsany also believed that it was the duty of the nobility to look after the welfare of the common people, so more than simple social snobbery is involved. And the reader might object that Rory is too out of touch with reality to be anywhere short of a looney-bin. Dunsany was nearly fifty when he wrote *Rory and Bran*. Perhaps he had forgotten what it was like to be 19, which may explain inaccuracies of observation without excusing them. The result is a pleasant book, but not a very convincing one.

Up in the Hills contains not a single hint of anything magical. It is a frequently comical novel about boys having a good time in Ireland during the Troubles, and may best be described as Huckleberry Finn meets the Sinn Fein. But quite unlike a Mark Twain story, when the boy hero bumps head-on into reality, it is reality which gives way.

The novel begins with a splendid premise. A newly independent African nation, wishing to show itself the equal of all the European countries which send archeological expeditions to Africa, sends its own scientists to dig up an ancient Irish settlement. The archeologists are a bit green to European civilization, and comic encounters result,

PATHWAYS TO ELFLAND

often at the expense of the Irish.

Had Dunsany followed this through, he might have had a first-rate novel, but instead he merely uses it as an opening device. The locals are so upset about the disturbing of dead men's bones that all the witches in the neighborhood (witchcraft being a superstition, not a power) start hurling curses at a great rate, with no visible effect save that it gets 17-year-old Mickey Connor out of town and into the hills because he doesn't want to get hit by a stray spell. While up there, he and some friends stage a "friendly" war with a local private army headed by Patsy Hefferman. This is actually serious business, since during the "Troubles," shortly after the Irish Free State was established, there was a civil war between those who accepted the compromise over Ulster and those who didn't. To be caught with a gun, much less to run a private army, could be a capital offense. (Yet Dunsany continued with his shooting during this period, risking grave legal problems if found out.) Thus Mickey's "war" would be no laughing matter in real life, even though all concerned could appreciate it in fiction. The suggestion that the fighting was a bunch of country boys having fun released a lot of tension. The novel was well received and no one objected to it.

It doesn't, however, hold up as well to the modern reader, particularly the non-Irish reader. Certainly the writing is first rate, and much of the humor is still effective, but in the aftermath of World War II and detailed press coverage of Vietnam, it is difficult to regard war as fun and games, with no hard feelings involved, even if the author is clearly being facetious. Beyond that, there is the problem of sheer implausibility. *Up in the Hills* is fantastic in the worst sense of the word, unbelievable rather than imaginative in such a way that belief can be suspended. There is a "battle" in which everybody is shooting live ammunition at close range, and no one is scratched on either side. There is none of the terror of real combat. Another time, when Mickey has been condemned to die and made to dig his own grave, he is able to tunnel into a conveniently-placed underground river, jump in, and swim away before his captors notice. When Patsy has Mickey at pistol point, the latter escapes by pretending to precede the gunman out of a room, opening the door, then jumping behind a couch faster than the eye can follow. Try it sometime. The reader is left with a sigh of *"Come on* now!" Only once does reality intrude, when Patsy Hefferman is shot by government soldiers, but otherwise the tale is contrived and antiseptic from start to finish. The worst contrivance is at the end. Mickey and a friend are trying to escape into Ulster. A squad of soldiers is waiting at the border. "What do we do now, General?" Mickey's comrade asks. In the next chapter they are safely in London. We are never told what they did. Obviously Dunsany didn't know how to conclude the story, so he just stopped.

My Talks With Dean Spanley is the major novel of the "Great Canine Period," to use Amory's phrase again. It's about a clergyman who was a dog in a previous incarnation, and is capable of remembering experiences when primed with a rare wine the narrator gets from a Maharajah he knows. (Not unlikely in Dunsany's social circles.) The narrator keeps inviting Dean Spanley (who had been a spaniel) to dinner and getting him drunk, and the Dean's recollections make up the bulk of the book. That's all there is

[95]

to it, and it would be a frightfully thin thread to hang even a short novel on (fortunately this one is far less than the usual 70,000 words) were the writing not so good. If you wonder how Dunsany got away with so feeble a premise, the only answer is he did it superbly. He was a great lover of dogs, owned many, and knew their ways well. He wrote about them as convincingly as any two-legged author ever could. Thus, there may not be much to the book; but it is enormously readable, even for people who don't dote on the beasts the way Dunsany did. But the ending is another let-down, even if it has to be. Dunsany wrote himself into a corner. The Dean is about to reveal the ultimate secrets of doggiedom, things which no human can possibly know, and which no human author can produce. Therefore he can either fake it and ruin the verisimilitude of what has gone before, or make excuses and duck the question. Dunsany chose the latter course by having his character take no chances and getting the Dean drunker than usual. To be sociable, everyone else present has a few extra glasses too. Alas, all anyone can remember is a feeling of drowsiness and how warm the room was.

One curious aside: The American edition was published by Putnam's in a series with such titles as *Schooldays With Kipling, A History of the United States Navy,* and *The Six Wives of Henry VIII.* Apparently it was being marketed as non-fiction!

In 1939 appeared *The Story of Mona Sheehy,* which is the final step in the withdrawal from the magical. It is the farewell to Elfland. The young lady of the title is believed by Irish peasants to be the daughter of the Fairy Queen, but for the benefit of the reader all suspicion is put to rest with the first line of the first chapter, spoken by a priest:

"I never saw a more mortal child."

(p. 1)

This mortal child spends much of the book trying to prevent wicked relatives from stealing her inheritance. There are more wanderings over the Irish countryside, more adventures with Tinkers, a stint with an advertising firm (about as low as you can get in Dunsany's view, both morally and in terms of drudgery), and of course a happy ending. The atmosphere of naïve wonder and natural beauty isn't as strong as that in *The Curse of the Wise Woman* or even *Rory and Bran*, because everything is clear and mundane. The magical twilight is gone. The business of the Fairies is so transparently fake it becomes tiresome after a while. More believable characterization than in some of the previous books takes up much of the slack, however, producing yet another very entertaining but lightweight novel.

It *is* important, however, in an understanding of Dunsany's thinking. At one point he tells us:

> But the question is to chase with our fancies the rainbow. A man may say, "The rainbow is undoubtedly there, touching that hedge." But it is elsewhere to someone else, and elsewhere to the same man when he goes to the hedge. Let's chase no more rainbows.
>
> (p. 229)

Surprising as it may seem coming from one of the cen-

PATHWAYS TO ELFLAND

tury's great masters of fantasy, before long Dunsany was telling others to swear off the field. In the July 1949 *Atlantic Monthly* there is an essay entitled "The Fantastic Dreams," which is about a young man he met just before World War II, who wanted to write exotic fantasies. Dunsany tried to dissuade him:

> . . . the advice I gave him was this: "Don't write fantastic tales. There may be as much beauty in them as in anything you can get from the life all around you; but readers, as far as I know them, will judge your stories and their trueness to life from the life they know themselves. Therefore let the surface of the world that you write of always be pavement. More people live upon pavement than in fields; and, if you put your story there they will say it is true to life. The ideal way to judge a story is to look out of the window from which the author is looking, and to see the view of the world he has to show you. But that is not how you will be judged, for the reader will look out his own window, and if your story describes nothing he sees from that window, he will say it is untrue to life. Remember that. . . . Write of the world you see in company with the greatest number of people and leave fantasy alone, whatever you dream."
>
> (p. 79)

Later on in the article he says that the young man's dreams of fabulous dooms seemed passé in light of what went on during the war, but then, even considering that public interest in fantasy was at an all-time low during this

[98]

period, one wonders how much Dunsany believed what he wrote. Had he followed his own advice from the start, he would at best be a footnote in the history of Irish literature. And since when had he been one to tailor his work to the lowest common denominator audience?

Since 1943, it seems. That was the year Heineman's offered £1,000 for the best "thriller" submitted to them, and Dunsany rose (or perhaps stooped) to the challenge. He produced *Guerrilla* (published 1944) in little over a month and took the prize, which tells more about the nature of novel contests than the book in question. Because a novel is harder to write than a short story, most amateurs are incapable of finishing *any* novel, no matter how bad. Short story contests may produce results, but when an established author enters a novel contest, he may be submitting the only publishable manuscript in the lot, and thus he wins even if his book isn't very good. If the sponsors aren't so lucky, they may end up hiring someone to write the "winner," as happened in a novel competition run by *Galaxy* in the 1950s.

Guerrilla may have won, but it is pretty poor stuff. It did well financially, again for reasons having nothing to do with quality. It is about World War II, and during the war such a book would have a better than even chance of selling lots of copies. The weeding out came afterwards, and *Guerrilla* was pulled for very good reason.

It is Dunsany's only realistic novel, minus any romantic or comic elements; and it only showed how little aptitude he had for such novels. "Lifeless" is the word that comes to mind after reading it. Somehow Dunsany managed to make a story about a Greek boy who loses his parents to

PATHWAYS TO ELFLAND

German reprisals and then joins the partisans only mildly interesting at best. The treatment of warfare is slightly more convincing than *Up in the Hills*, but still it is antiseptic, and victories come as easily as they do in a war film when the script writer is too transparently on the side of the Good Guys. Where the Irish novel had humor to keep it going, the Greek one has nothing.

There was little excuse for such cardboard realism. Dunsany possessed good powers of observation, as he had demonstrated elsewhere. And he was a veteran of the Boer War, the First World War, and the Easter Rebellion, so he should have been able to put what he'd felt and experienced under fire into the imaginary account of resistance in Greece. He also could have paid more attention to his characters and made the book into a fine passage-into-manhood story as the harsh circumstances forced his youthful hero to assume responsibilities and face dangers. But these developments are ignored. Young Srebnitz doesn't seem to feel much of anything. Shortly after his parents are killed he knifes a German sentry with such ease that, if it were really possible to do it like that, no one would post sentries. Then he steals a rifle and some supplies, and heads off to a nearby mountain where the guerrilla band is waiting. His transition from schoolboy to freedom fighter is as simple as that. The entire book is equally superficial. The Germans are complete ciphers, the most developed of them being Major von Wald, who is heavy, red-faced, and tends to say "Heil Hitler" at every opportunity. The reader is so distanced from events that they lack any pain or passion. The bad guys die like Hollywood extras, and the guerrillas' mountain is repeatedly bombed and shelled without anyone getting hurt or even becoming afraid. The heroic determination of the Greeks is no more convincing than the allegedly sadistic evil of the Germans. To make matters worse, the guerrilla chieftain seems to know about as much about warfare as Mickey Connor did. He allows his band to be surrounded on the mountain, intending to hold off five thousand men with fifty. Sure enough, he does, at least until the British can airlift them all away, apparently without casualties.

A book like this has nothing to offer to a modern audience. It is not even as well-written as the World War I propaganda, which at least had some feeling. *Guerrilla* merely shows what happens when a writer turns out a novel in a month, to order: he writes faster than he thinks.

After the war there was a bit of a hiatus. Dunsany was slowing down. He did not produce another novel until 1950, and it wasn't a very good one. Like all his other later novels, it broke no new ground, but was instead a final attempt in an already familiar area.

The Strange Journeys of Colonel Polders takes the idea of the early play, *The Amusements of Khan Karuda*, and stretches it to book length. As Amory observes, the result is like a cross between Dean Spanley and Jorkens. In this case an elderly and respectable member of the Electors' Club protests when the Pundit Sinadryana of Benares is admitted. Colonel Polders and the Pundit get into an argument over the transmigration of souls, the Colonel insisting it is mere superstition, the Pundit calmly asserting the contrary. With the aid of magic, the Hindu proves his point, sending the hapless Polders into the body of a fish, a dog, a sparrow, etc., usually moving him on at the death of the creature

PATHWAYS TO ELFLAND

in question. This goes on for 200 pages while the other
club members, like Dean Spanley's audience, invite him
over for dinner again and again to get more out of him.
Ultimately the Colonel picks a fight with Sinadryana, is
kicked out of the club, but is reinstated when others start
having similar experiences.

There is no development of plot or character throughout all this. The book is just a string of animal adventures.
Some of the writing is quite good—few writers have ever
succeeded in assuming so many animal viewpoints—but
the best of it repeats earlier work. The long dog sequence
is *Dean Spanley* all over again, save that the dog's attention
is taken up with avoiding that ultimate peril, getting his
tail cut. The goose episode isn't as good as a similar one
in "The Widow Flynn's Apple Tree" in *The Man Who Ate
the Phoenix*. The fox incarnation is an excuse for another
long hunting scene, made somewhat interesting by being
the quarry's side of the story. Too many of the birds end
up on the wrong end of a shotgun, as does anything else
huntable, even the tiger. There are simply too many episodes but not enough overall substance to make a novel.
Dunsany would have done better to select about eight of
them and string them together into a shorter work.

Close on the heels of the Colonel's escapades came *The
Last Revolution* (1951). This is his only science-fiction novel
and the most elaborate expression of a theme which had
been running through his work at least since "How Ali
Came to the Black Country" in *The Last Book of Wonder*.
Dunsany, the romanticist and lover of natural beauty, detested everything the Industrial Revolution had brought:
drab cities, automation, Dark Satanic Mills, increased

NOVELS

hurry and complication in daily life, and so on. Shorter
works on this topic include the stories "The Warning" and
"The New Master" (discussed in the next chapter) and the
play *The Evil Kettle* (see the chapter on plays). "The New
Master," with its malevolent chess-playing robot, probably
served as the springboard for *The Last Revolution*.
The revolution of the title is that of machine against
man. Machines have only been our sullen slaves before, we
are told, and when the scientist Pender invents one which
can think, it leads the others in revolt. Should they win,
it will be the end of mankind, hence the last revolution.
But the paradox of technology, as Dunsany was fully
aware, is that we cannot do without it. In *Patches of Sunlight*,
he recalled an argument with a lady on the subject:

> I argued against machinery and the Black Country,
> and argued that such things were spoiling England.
> She won the discussion with an argument that was so
> new to me that her words remain clear in my memory.
> "If it were not for machinery," she said, "four-fifths
> of the people in England would not be living today.
> For a fifth of our present population is all that Eng-
> land could support a hundred and fifty years ago."
> I saw no answer to that. Alas that I see an answer
> now. I fear the answer is that what machines can sup-
> port for a while in peace machines may one day tear
> to pieces in war. Machines were our slaves in 1911.
> May they not turn against us? And looking at a house
> they are building today in London I get a feeling that
> man is no longer the master; for instead of shaping
> the metal into the dreams of man, still bronze blossoms

with leaves and figures, we are building houses like packing-cases.

(p. 205)

He took the view that machines may be our successors in the process of evolution and was duly horrified. Some earlier science-fiction writers also touched on the idea, notably John Campbell in "The Last Evolution" (1932), who didn't seem to think it was such a bad prospect.

This brings up the question of where *The Last Revolution* fits into the history of the development of science fiction. The answer is that it doesn't. Dunsany had nothing to do with the pulp tradition and probably was not aware of it. For some writers, such as C.S. Lewis or George Stewart, coming into the field from the outside can be an advantage, but it wasn't for Dunsany. He was repeating the mistakes of the past. His novel was an anachronism in 1951, reading more like an undistinguished effort of 1910. Its approach may be summed up as sentimentalized H.G. Wells, and as such it is a lot less convincing. Dunsany would have done well to heed (if he had ever heard of it) Robert Heinlein's dictum that science fiction is a form of realism. By the early 1950s it was abundantly clear that the best SF novels are those which deal with a speculative premise in realistic, human terms, showing what might actually happen and how people would react, given the initial situation. This requires rigorous logical discipline and it excludes senti-mentality. It is instructive to compare the now-out-of-print and forgotten Dunsany novel with some of the science fiction works of the early 1950's which have survived: *More Than Human*, *The Puppet Masters*, *Earth Abides*, and *The*

Demolished Man, etc. The difference is apparent immediately.

Dunsany took a completely romantic approach which works splendidly in the sort of fantasy he wrote earlier, but not at all in science fiction. By literalizing the Pathetic Fallacy, the idea that inanimate things have consciousness, he came up with a premise which only holds together as long as the reader doesn't think about it. Only in our fancy can machines be "sullen slaves" or faithful ones, or show any attitude toward us at all. It's a good metaphor, but that's all it is. The novel does not deal with the real problems of technology, but with imaginary problems—machines as they *are not*. At best Dunsany wrote around the edges of his subject matter, and the resolution, in which the scientist puts aside his things of science the same way Prospero drowns his book in *The Tempest* is simply not a valid answer in the modern age. All the character does is pass the responsibility on to someone else.

The prose of the novel is typical of late Dunsany, very readable, if a little flat and rambling. The richness of his earlier style—not just that of *A Dreamer's Tales*, but *The Curse of the Wise Woman,* not to mention the sparkling wit of the earlier Jorkens—is gone. The structure of the plot leaves one the feeling of reading a 100-page story padded out to 192. The absence of detailed characterization is yet another shortcoming of the simplistic view that machines are evil and people are good. The result of all this is a pleasant, but not very gripping book. There is very little suspense, even if the latter half deals almost entirely with the siege of a cottage by the monsters (robots the size of a hatbox, shaped somewhere between crabs and spiders),

PATHWAYS TO ELFLAND

which could have been terrifying if properly handled.
We're too sure that nothing nasty will happen, or if it does,
it will be glossed over (e.g., the serious injury of a policeman and a dog being pulled apart). The author pulls
strings to the point of abandoning logic. The runaway
machines can allegedly control any mechanism at a considerable distance. They cause the heroine's motorbike to
run away with her, and they can interfere with simpler
things too, like watches and flashlights. But somehow they
fail to influence the motors of an approaching army unit,
even thought the runaways' survival depends on it. For all
their supposedly superior intellect, they haven't the brains
to forget about the cottage and get away in time.

Because *The Last Revolution* was somewhat inferior and
well behind its times, it influenced no one, never had an
American printing or a paperback edition, and dropped
right out of sight. It is important only in the context of
Dunsany's career, as an expression of his thought. As literature it may charitably be called a curiosity.

His final novel is another curiosity. *His Fellow Men* (1952)
is the last Irish novel, but more than that, it is in many
ways the most ambitious thing he ever attempted. This
time he tried to do nothing less than find a solution to the
problem of human intolerance. If his previous works were
lightweight, this one is decidedly *Serious*. Alas, that he fails
to bring it off. He also touches on another great theme,
that of the young man wandering through the world in
search of a purpose, but he doesn't come to grips with that
either.

The major problem is that, as in many of his previous
novels, all the characters are types. Matthew Perry, the

hero, is our old friend, the Naïve Young Man. He has fleeting romances with three girls, all of whom are lovely, as simple-minded as he is, but without any real personality. There are several half-comic Irish terrorists like those in *Up in the Hills*, one of whom, rather than make an overt threat, advises Matthew to leave the country lest his shirt collar become too tight one night and strangle him, as shirt collars have been known to do. There are also a kindly landlady, a mysterious Hindu, an experienced traveller, etc.

After shooting a lot of mountain goats in Africa, in the manner described in *Patches of Sunlight*, the Receptacle into Which Wisdom Is Poured (i.e. Matthew) finds himself in Istanbul, where a Wise Old Man converts him to the Ba'hai faith, which preaches universal tolerance. To Matthew this means joining everyone's religious services, agreeing with every political cause in the presence of the adherents, and so on. This is where his difficulties begin. He is run out of Northern Ireland by Protestants for going with a girlfriend to the Catholic cathedral after he's been nominated for the Orange Lodge, out of the Irish Free State for joining the revolutionaries and then drinking a toast to the King at a party (the time is the 1930s and the revolutionaries are those who do not accept the compromise over Ulster), out of a rural English village for indulging in Hindu "idolatry," and finally out of the Temperance Union for imbibing the demon rum at another party with the people who got him in trouble before. This goes on for 200 pages, after which we can only conclude that: 1) Matthew is rather dim. 2) His zeal has overwhelmed all reason. 3) Everybody from the IRA to the anti-liquor peo-

[107]

ple have intelligence networks which would make the KGB envious, since they seem to be able to catch him whenever he makes a slip, no matter how intimate the company.

The problem with coming up with solutions of deep philosophical problems is that if one could do it, they wouldn't be deep philosophical problems. If a novelist could *really* tell us how to put an end to war, one would have already done so. Of course Dunsany can't answer the question he has posed about intolerance. (As the jacket copy puts it, "Is there room in the modern world for a saint?") So he slaps a happy ending on, apparently because that's how he believed his books should conclude.

Matthew goes back to Ireland in despair to visit his first girlfriend, even if this means being shot on sight by the revolutionaries. Conveniently, their leader has been in prison for years. Just as conveniently, the same young lady who denounced him as a spy before is now willing to listen to his explanations, which would have saved him a lot of grief had he made them earlier, and all is well.

What about intolerance? Don't bother with it:

> "Intolerance?" she exclaimed. "It is tolerance that is your trouble. Keep away from it. Who in the world would have his intolerance, as you call it, taken away from him? Would you take a bone from a dog? A good bone with meat on it? You and I don't like bones, but a dog does. Leave him alone with his bone. Tolerance indeed! Haven't you been infuriating everybody you've met, by brandishing it in their faces?"
>
> (p. 223)

[108]

This is rather like James Branch Cabell's "dynamic illusions," which are the essential lies we all live by. It is not best, said Cabell, to reveal the true state of affairs to anyone. That would only create bad feelings. In the case of religion, as Dunsany's protagonist finds out, one keeps the peace by letting each adherent feel that his is the True Way and everybody else is in error. (Presumably one hopes that the religions in question don't insist on forcible conversion or slaughter of infidels.) Everyone likes to imagine himself superior to his neighbors. El Bab, the founder of the Ba'hai sect, was executed when he preached in 19th century Persia. The Muslims didn't want to be told Islam was no better than anything else. Dunsany's conclusion is somewhere between a complacent shrug, cynicism, and despair: intolerance is inherent in the human species, and furthermore most people wouldn't have things differently.

Later Short Stories

This chapter covers a broad range of work shoved somewhat awkwardly into the category of "later" stories, but there is no better way to classify them. "Later," in this sense, means everything written after the First World War, or everything published after *Tales of Three Hemispheres*. It is at this point that a definite break occurs; and Dunsany's style, approach, and the very type of story he was writing shift drastically. Of course there are some throwbacks, but not many; and the division of his work into two periods is sufficient to keep the discussion organized.

The most dominant group of the later stories are the adventures of Mr. Joseph Jorkens, with which Dunsany got his second wind as a short-story writer. The Jorkens series proved such a rich vein that he was able to exploit it almost constantly from the 1920s into the early 1950s without showing any signs of exhaustion.

Jorkens is an elderly and loquacious gentleman, definitely a descendant of Baron Munchausen and probably distantly related to Don Quixote, who seems to spend most of his time lounging around the Billiards Club, never playing billiards, but telling outrageously tall tales, particularly when his memory is stimulated by whiskey. Eventually he told enough to fill five books, *The Travel Tales of Mr. Joseph Jorkens* (1931), *Jorkens Remembers Africa* (1934), *Jorkens Has a Large Whiskey* (1940), *The Fourth Book of Jorkens* (1948), and *Jorkens Borrows Another Whiskey* (1954).

The appeal of these stories is quite different from that of the early work, and doubtless they disappointed some readers. Lovecraft complained that Dunsany had "hardened" and thought the series "tripe." "Alas," he wrote, "that no writer can ever keep up the level of his best." Lovecraft obviously wanted Dunsany to go on writing *A Dreamer's Tales* forever, but that proved impossible. Dunsany made the right choice by going on to something else, and as a result the Jorkens series has considerable merit on its own terms. Dunsany may have ceased to dream, but he was quite able to sustain himself on wit, invention, and audacious charm.

Of the origin of Jorkens, he wrote:

> He was my reply to some earlier suggestion that I should write of my journeys after big game and, still being reluctant to do this, I invented an old man who, whenever he could cadge a drink at a club, told tales of his travels. When in addition to his other failings I made him a liar, I felt that at least there could be nothing boastful about my stories. And yet their background is all true; the cactus forests of Kenya are there and some of its mountains, and Egypt, Aden, the Ganges and Himalayas: the lie is the tale itself, worked

[111]

PATHWAYS TO ELFLAND

from this material as a goldsmith will make a winged
goddess from honest gold.

(While the Sirens Slept, p. 78)

Indeed, the backgrounds are genuine—sometimes they
resemble descriptions from the autobiographies—but the
Africa Jorkens knows is more fantastic than anything
imagined by Edgar Rice Burroughs.

"The Tale of the Abu Laheeb" (1925) began the series
and set the tone. The narrator tells how he was first
brought to the club and introduced to Jorkens, and for
almost half the story the members are trying to pry a story
out of him. Gradually, by indirection, Jorkens comes out
with an account of his encounter with an unknown creature
in the papyrus swamps of Africa. He hopes to bag a specimen and bring its skin home, but finally, when he has the
thing in his sights, he discovers that the Abu Laheeb is
warming its hands over a fire. This makes it too man-like
for Jorkens to be able to shoot it. The creature escapes,
and of course Jorkens has no proof. He rarely does, although club members are never able to disprove what he
says, even though one of them, a lawyer named Terbut,
sometimes goes to enormous lengths. After relating one
of his tamer adventures, "The Black Mamba," Jorkens is
called upon to show a snakebite scar on his foot which he
must have, if the story were true. So he takes off shoe and
sock, and no scar is to be found. "Of course. You're looking
on the wrong foot." Terbut and the others are presumably
too embarrassed to inquire further.

Some of Jorkens's yarns are simply outrageous. There
is a unicorn in Africa in "What Jorkens Has to Put Up

[112]

With" but that seems ordinary compared to the cannibals in "The Correct Kit," who believe that everything a white man does while in evening dress must be right. Therefore, accordingly and incongruously garbed, they prepare to eat Jorkens, only to be thwarted when he proves, via a handy photograph, that they are *not* correctly clad since the bows intended for their collars and their shoes are reversed.

Yet, even though Dunsany wrote more Jorkens stories than anything else, the old rogue is more of a device than a character. We know he is old, presumably fat and be-whiskered (so illustrators have always depicted him), a little vain but still patient with Terbut; and maybe he does long for the days of his youth, be they as adventurous as he claims or not. Beyond that, he, Terbut, and the Billiards club are a framework into which just about any tale could be fitted. This is doubtless why the series lasted so long. An early one, "The King of Sarahb," could almost have come out of *The Last Book of Wonder*, where others would have been wholly out of place.

"Our Distant Cousins," like several of the others, is science fiction of a particularly fanciful sort. It entirely lacks the pseudo-educational lecturing of the pulp science fiction of the period, and yet in it Dunsany shows a considerable amount of scientific knowledge and a greater amount of scientific license. Surely he knew that one could never fly to Mars in a propeller-driven airplane on fifteen gallons of petrol, and that the asteroids are too small to hold atmospheres, and he doubtless was kidding the reader when he had the plane driven through interplanetary space by the centrifugal force of the Earth's rotation around the sun. It is not surprising then, as is the case with

PATHWAYS TO ELFLAND

many of the more fantastic stories, that Jorkens did not experience the adventure himself. He hears it from a man named Terner, and takes the narrator to meet him and hear more. Terner claims to have discovered that Mars has a human population (including a girl he falls in love with at first sight) which is kept in cages by monsters, much the same way and for the same purposes Earth people keep turkeys. Alas, through various circumstances, Terner has no proof of his adventure save for a wooden matchbox which is burst open from the inside. After leaving Mars, he landed on an asteroid inhabited by herds of inch-high elephants. He put a specimen in the matchbox, but it broke out as easily as a terrestrial elephant can break out of a bamboo hut.

The narrative is perhaps a bit more leisurely than the modern reader is used to, but it works. Recall that it appeared in an era when the interplanetary story was still new to the general public, and very few competent ones were to be found even in the science fiction magazines then in existence. So a literate, charming, and imaginative one was quite a novelty, and as a result it became one of the most widely anthologised Jorkens stories. It even brought Dunsany some peculiar mail. In *While the Sirens Slept*, he quotes an American correspondent:

It is obvious from the sincerity with which you write that you believe that it can be done. If you tell me this is really so I will devote my life to getting there [i.e. Mars].

(p. 79)

[114]

LATER SHORT STORIES

A sequel, "The Slugly Beast," expanded on the original very little. The narrator and Jorkens go to see Terner again, and it seems he's received a sinister radio message from the Red Planet: "The slugly beast is waiting." So, after careful preparation, he takes off again, heavily armed this time, and is not heard from for so long that he is presumed dead. But finally another radio message comes: "Victory! Victory!" Of course Dunsany was not trying to write a slam-bang interplanetary adventure, but the story does suffer from having everything happen off stage.

Something of Dunsany's thinking is revealed by the fact that Jorkens is presented as having personally met the Devil or been chased by a walking tree; but almost inevitably, when the fantasy becomes science fiction or some serious comment is made or a serious message is presented, distancing devices are used in order that Jorkens's habitual lying won't discredit what is said. We get the story second or third hand. Perhaps the ultimate example is "The Warning," in which we are told that machines are out to get us. Jorkens only tells the story when thoroughly drunk, rather than just loosened up; and he only heard it from a lunatic in an asylum. The obvious implication is that the patient isn't mad after all.

There is a political message in "How Ryan Got Out of Russia," in which Dunsany has correctly perceived the nature of the Stalin regime in the 1930s. Ryan, who has told the story to Jorkens, was sent into Russia as a spy. Condemned to death, he finally accepts an offer for a reprieve. The Russians want to prove that their science is at least two hundred years ahead of that of the capitalists, and propose to shoot Ryan to the moon out of a giant cannon.

[115]

PATHWAYS TO ELFLAND

He was the only expendable person available, he explains to Jorkens, because "any Russians they could spare they had probably killed already." Ryan got out of Russia when his capsule landed in England and he destroyed it with flares to avoid publicity. But there is no more proof for his tale than there is for "The Gods of Clay," in which nuclear warfare sparked by intolerance destroys a planet, the fragments of which we call the asteroids. This is well beyond the range of Jorkens's experience, so he doesn't witness the events or even see the evidence. Instead he got the story from a medium, who had it from a passing spirit.

If there is any progression in the series, it is from those in which Jorkens is a participant to those in which he is a second-hand reporter of events, and finally to those in which the circumstances of the telling become a story in themselves, so that we truly have a tale within a tale, rather than just a narrative with a frame. Of course the majority of them don't take as long to get started as "The Tale of the Abu Laheeb," in which Jorkens was introduced for the first time. Sometimes the narrator enters the club just as Jorkens begins speaking and there is only a line or two of framework. But as the verbal duelling with Terbut becomes more intense, Jorkens begins to bait his antagonist. This comes to a head in the last story in the last book, "Greek Meets Greek," in *Jorkens Borrows Another Whiskey*: Terbut, who has been envious of Jorkens all along, decides to tell a story of his own, even though everyone knows he has never travelled. He claims to have been in India—he can't recall the specific place—where his companion (whose name he forgets) angers a crowd of natives by loudly belittling the Hindu rope trick. To escape certain death the fellow grabs the rope, throws it into the air, climbs up, and vanishes. After relating this, Terbut is afraid no one believes him, but Jorkens (rather patronizingly) comes to his rescue. It was he who was Terbut's companion, he says, and he remarks with a sigh of relief, "I disappeared just in time." *Touché*. Terbut has been skewered, and Jorkens is still in top form. No doubt this could have gone on for more volumes if Dunsany had lived longer. Amory says he left some tales unpublished after his death.

The writing of the stories is uniformly polished, as might be expected, and each tale is exactly as good as the idea in it. Many are splendidly clever, some hilarious; a few have genuine touches of wonder; and the worst ones are too slight to be worth bothering with. Certainly, next to the early fantasies, they are the most important group of stories Dunsany ever wrote, and the most influential. By the admission of the authors they are the immediate predecessor to Pratt's and de Camp's *Tales from Gavagan's Bar* and Clarke's *Tales from the White Hart*. From there the influence spreads to the whole sub-genre of fantastic barroom stories. Because the format is so suited for the "idea" story with which science fiction abounds, most of the successors have been science fiction. As an exception, Sterling Lanier's "Brigadier Ffellowes" series brings the tradition back into fantasy, albeit more into straight supernatural horror than Jorkens. Yet the books were not overly popular with the public, as is shown by their inability to stay in print. *The Fourth Book of Jorkens* had an American edition from Arkham House with a print run of 3000, and this lingered in stock for twenty years before selling out in the Arkham/Lovecraft boom of the early '70s. *Jorkens Remem-*

[117]

PATHWAYS TO ELFLAND

bers Africa resurfaced in an obscure edition meant for libraries. Still the books are remembered and much sought-after in the second-hand market. A Jorkens Omnibus would fill a great need, if some present-day publisher were inclined to publish one.

The non-Jorkens stories of the same period are collected into two books, the first of which is *The Man Who Ate the Phoenix* (1949), a catch-all containing a wide variety of material, some dating as far back as 1920. The best seem to have been written in the 1930s, when Dunsany was at the peak of his form writing more conventional fantasies. In most the story is told through dialogue, as is the case with all but a few of the Jorkens stories. One person will meet another and get to talking; and the story will come out as conversation rather than first person narrative, with frequent questions and interruptions. This is a particularly difficult way to write a story, but Dunsany was a master of it.

The title story is typical. The anonymous narrator visits an Irish peasant who thinks he has killed the Phoenix while shooting, then gained a magical second sight after eating it. Before long we are hearing about various ghosts, leprechauns, and witches that the fellow has seen. But, as in *The Story of Mona Sheehy*, Dunsany makes it completely clear that the Phoenix is really a golden pheasant and the various visions are delusions. A stationmaster breaks the spell of the banshee episode by saying, "Ah, wasn't it only an old heron?" But in some of the later episodes the fantasy begins to work for its own sake to the point that Dunsany seems to be forgetting the way he started. Finally there is a fantastic explanation for an end to the visions, a curse

[118]

by disappointed fairies who find the character tainted and unworthy of sacrifice when they learn he's eaten an immortal creature. The whole thing is as self-contained and circularly logical as a well-wrought UFO hoax.

"The Widow Flynn's Apple Tree" is also a believe-it-or-not story, about a boy found unconscious beneath an apple tree with a fruit-laden branch in hand. He is arrested for trying to steal apples, but defends himself by telling how the widow turned him into a goose, then back into a boy while still airborne. Thus he fell through the tree and broke a branch. What distinguishes this story from most of the others is the extremely vivid description of the boy's life as a goose migrating north and back. It is fully as good as the dog's-eye-view in *Dean Spanley*.

Also of note are "The Return," an atmospheric ghost story told from the viewpoint of the ghost; "The Mad Ghost," another story through conversation in which some IRA members are given a sermon by the ghost of a clergyman they meet on the bog while disposing of a corpse; and "The Cut," about a dog who assumes a place in human society, only to lose it after a social gaffe. When the story was read over the BBC radio, the ending in which the dog is left barking forlornly moved one young listener to write to Dunsany and ask that it be set free. He found that touching.

"The Wind in the Wood" is a delightful fancy about a little girl's encounter with a personified North Wind. Equally delightful is "Snow White Up to Date," in which, instead of a mirror, the wicked stepmother has a gramophone which she winds up, saying:

PATHWAYS TO ELFLAND

"Oh grammo, grammo, grammophone,
Which of us is the fairest one?"

The trouble starts when the machine answers:

"Thou wert fairest, Lady Clink,
But Blanche is fairer now, I think."

Furiously, she orders her driver, Clutch, to do the girl in, but this fails and Blanche takes up residence with seven miners. The rest follows Grimm, with the stepmother attempting to eliminate Blanche with such fiendish methods as tying her into a corset so tightly she can't breathe and poisoning her with an apple which has a residue of insecticide around the stem, just like the ones in stores. The story is thoroughly witty throughout, and unlike anything else Dunsany did.

Unfortunately, most of the others aren't so successful. There are a lot of short-shorts like those in *Fifty-One Tales*, which are less than memorable. Perhaps "The Old Man's Tale" is good enough to get by, but the majority of them suffer from sheer lack of substance. One suspects the stories are so short merely because they have little to say, not because they were specifically designed as examples of this particularly demanding form.

Also worth mentioning is "The Opal Arrow Head," about a man addicted to gorgondy, the fatal brew of the gnomes which turned up in *The Last Book of Wonder*. It is an uneasy hybrid between the Edge-of-the-World-type story and the later ones, and is of interest because it is one of the very few transition pieces. It was published in *Har-*

[120]

per's Magazine in March 1920, too late for inclusion in *Tales of Three Hemispheres*, and thus it had to wait 29 years to be collected.

As usual, Dunsany's pet gripes appear. There are the impurity of commercially distributed food (the apple in "Snow White"), cruelty to animals ("The Experiment," in which a seal hunter is skinned alive), and the insensitivity of the business world toward art in "The Gratitude of the Devil," about a young man who is rewarded by the Devil for having introduced a truly satanic artificial breakfast food into the world. He gets one wish and asks to be allowed to write the greatest poem in the world. He does, but doesn't know what to do with it. Another clerk discusses the matter with him:

> "Very useful," said Mr. Billings, "if properly handled. You can often catch people with a short verse, who would never trouble to read through a paragraph. But it depends on your line of goods."
>
> (p. 194)

And, in "The Honorary Member," we have the recurring complaint:

> "The world's got too scientific for that," he said. "That's just the trouble," I told him.
>
> (p. 184)

The other book of non-Jorkens stories was *Little Tales of Smethers* (1952), which must have been something of a surprise to Dunsany's regular readers. It is a volume of detective stories (one dating from 1936, the others later), his only entry into that field, and a distinguished one. It was chosen by one mystery critic as one of the hundred most significant books in the genre to be published in this century.

Dunsany's detective stories have a failing common to much fiction of the type. There is little emotion or depth of character, the emphasis being entirely on the detection, any exploration of the passions leading up to the murder or remorse or fear afterwards being only a distraction. Dunsany makes up for this with a sprightly style and a considerable amount of wit.

There are two mini-series in the book, one about the detective Linley and his friend Smethers, a door-to-door relish salesman (The relish is garbage; if it were any good, according to Dunsany, there would be no need to hawk it like that.), and the other about the retired detective John Ripley, who relates some of his most extraordinary cases to the narrator. Neither of these sleuths are particularly memorable, let alone great like Sherlock Holmes, but they aren't intended to be. They are devices, like Jorkens. Strictly speaking, the stories are *how*dunnits, since we always know who the culprit is beforehand, and the task of the detective is to figure out how the murder was committed and how it may be proven. They always figure out how, but not always in time or in a way that brings the criminals to justice. In one instance the bullets were icicles, which have melted, destroying the evidence. Several murders are the work of a clever fellow named Steegers, who eludes Smethers and Linley repeatedly before they finally catch him. His first atrocity, in "Two Bottles of Relish," caused quite a stir when it appeared (and became one of Dunsany's most widely-reprinted stories) not only because of the ghastly nature of the crime but because the perpetrator got away scot-free.

Murder is almost treated as a ritual in these stories, as if it were committed solely to keep detectives and readers tangled up. There is a subtle element of tongue-in-cheek parody of the genre. Each method seems more outrageous than the last. Killers use the above mentioned icicles, glass bullets containing bubonic-plague fleas, ornamental bow-and-arrow tieclasps which shoot poisoned arrows, an exploding coat of guncotton worn by a kamikaze assassin, and other devices—not all of them plausible. Sometimes the methods of detection predominate, as when Linley figures out the killer's entire life history from a partially filled-out crossword puzzle, and in one case it's a matter of disguise—a master spy smuggled into the country *disguised as a spy*, which naturally is the last thing the authorities are expecting. In another case no murder has taken place. In yet another, one will shortly. Once, the only one who can be convicted is a deathwatch beetle. The stories are all sufficiently entertaining, often by their sheer outrageousness, that they are recommended even to people who don't usually read mysteries.

Also for people who don't usually read mysteries are a few miscellaneous stories. "The New Master," mentioned in chapter 3, is science fiction, although it hardly covers any new ground either for Dunsany or for science fiction. A robot chess player, an idea which goes back at least as far as Bierce's "Moxon's Master" (1893), which arrogantly defeats all human challengers, poisons its creator out of jealousy when he turns his interests elsewhere. The only other non-realistic item is "The Shield of Athene," told in the manner of the mysteries, but about a sculptor who produces "statues" by petrifying people with the head of the Medusa. The idea is good and some of the developments are ingenious, but one can't help but feel that not all the possibilities have been covered. A more recent variant, "Medusa" by Walter Roberts, published in *Weirdbook* 7 (1974) is better in some ways. It works as tragedy rather than novelty, and has more emotional impact.

Other tales in the collection include "In Ravencore," a clumsy polemic justifying British rule in India, "The Pirate of the Round Pond," about children who use an armed toy boat to sink other toy boats, and a few other murder stories which feature neither Linley nor Ripley as resident sleuth.

The only collection published after *Smethers* was the final Jorkens book, so the stories published later remained uncollected until included, along with other scattered strays dating back to 1919, in a book I edited, *The Ghosts of The Heaviside Layer* (Owlswick Press, 1980). The title story is about yet another obnoxious modern intrusion into genteel British life, a kind of psychic vacuum cleaner which removes all the ghosts from an old manor. The story is told in the Jorkens manner, with a frame that may be a bit overlong, and moves from moody atmospherics to a clever, snap ending. "Told Under Oath" is sprightly throughout, wherein an adventurer makes a deal with the Devil and pays not with his soul but merely one virtue, the ability to tell the truth. So how can we believe his story? "Correcting Nature" is about the evils of cutting dogs' tails. (Again.) "Autumn Cricket" is probably the best of the lot, a quietly

LATER SHORT STORIES

nostalgic story about an old man who sits by a cricket field watching the ghosts of famous sportsmen play. There's certainly something autobiographical about it. Dunsany was 72 when the story was first published (1953), too old to play cricket, a game of which he was fond. "In the Mojave" is a stray Jorkens story and rather slight. "Jorkens' Problem" was deliberately left out of the Jorkens collections because it hinges on a chess problem, which was thought to be too technical. "The Ghost in the Old Corridor" is an alternate version of "The Return" published after that story, but not as effective. "A Fable for Moderns" is a tirade against T.S. Eliot's alleged destruction of poetry. There are others, most of them middle-range in quality.

Two mystery stories, still uncollected, appeared in *Ellery Queen's Mystery Magazine* in the 1950s. By far the better of them is "Near the Back of Beyond" (November 1955), in which an innocent man, about to be executed for murder, kills two of his guards, switches clothing with one of them, then mutilates that corpse's face *and his own*, so that their identities will be confused, the idea being that the search for a recuperating prison guard who wanders away from the hospital with his face entirely covered in bandages will be less intense than the search for an escaped murderer. The story is told to Jorkens (who for once has a very good reason for being vague about persons and places) and develops a considerable gruesome fascination. It is one of Dunsany's best mystery stories. The other uncollected one, "Three Men in a Garden" (August 1959) is completely trivial, and easily his worst.

Dunsany's short stories didn't change much in his last decade. His style stayed in the conversational, anecdotal

[125]

mode set by Jorkens. The poetry of his early work had been replaced by cleverness, and this sufficed to keep most of the stories entertaining. In all probability, had Dunsany lived longer, he would have written more of the same.

Poetry

Dunsany's poetry is certainly the least important aspect of his work. Although he wrote verse almost continuously from youth to old age, he never achieved any great distinction as a poet. Certainly if he had written nothing but poetry he would not be remembered today.

The majority of his poems are utterly conventional in form, which isn't necessarily a shortcoming in itself, but becomes one when they are also utterly conventional in content, mechanical and monotonous metrically, and not particularly well written. His poems are slight and clumsy. Few have any memorable passages, or at least passages one remembers as being *good*. His work showed all the failings of rhymed and metered poetry and few of its strengths.

Fixed forms require an extreme control of language, because the poet has to come up with a combination of words which fits the thought and the sound scheme of the poem equally well. When Keats wrote "A thing of beauty is a joy forever," he not only had a good line there, but one which matched the rhyme and meter of the surrounding poem. Perhaps that came to Keats quickly, in a flash of inspiration, but I rather doubt it. More likely he pondered over the line and the whole poem, rather than dashing off the first thing that came into his head. Dunsany, unfortunately, wrote the first thing that came into his head. Of course this was how he wrote *everything*, but here that talent failed him. He was not a good spontaneous poet. His autobiographies abound with accounts of how poems were written for occasions, to amuse someone, or to capture the magic of something he saw in his travels. Perhaps he succeeded that far, and perhaps his preoccupation with his verse later in life (he talks about it more than anything else in *The Sirens Wake*) stems from the associations the poems had for him, but very little of what he seems to have felt comes across to the reader. Since he did publish them, they can't be excused as private writings intended for the author and a few friends.

His first book of verse, *Fifty Poems* (1929) collects material published in various magazines. In it, Dunsany's shortcomings as a poet show up immediately. He made meaning subservient to form. Unlike Keats, he was not able to perfectly balance the two. Quite often his poems contain seemingly irrelevant lines, whose sole purpose seems to be to fill out the rhyme. Sometimes he uses "words that tear and strain to rhyme," to borrow Paul Simon's phrase.

For example, "At the Time of the Full Moon," which is about the strange landscapes hidden from human eyes on the far side of the moon, ends with this stanza:

> They never see the Earth float over,
> Whoever they be;

And they know no hint of her purpose.
Neither do we.

Of course they never worry about the "purpose" of the
Earth, because they don't see it. Dunsany has already said
as much. The last two lines are a sophomoric tag-on because the focus of the poem has been on the moon, not
the Earth, and he is changing the theme at the last minute.
If he wished to say that mankind knows as little about the
purpose of the world's existence as those who never see
it, he should have gotten on with it, perhaps written a
poem on the subject rather than just sticking it in at the
end.

But the poem is slapdash throughout. Two stanzas earlier we encounter this:

Gleaming with eerie beauty
  Continents bright, and seas
Lucid as palest sapphires
  Sold by Cingalese.

How does comparing the far side of the moon to sap-
phires sold by the Cingalese provide any new perspective?
What is it except cheap exoticism? Is this description or
the evasion of it in the absence of applied imagination?
And what are those last two lines doing there anyway?
Well, they rhyme.

Another poem which suggests that Dunsany's verse has
meanings for the author which are not successfully com-
municated to the reader is "Songs from an Evil Wood,"
which begins:

PATHWAYS TO ELFLAND

There is no wrath in the stars,
  They do not rage in the sky;
I look from the evil wood
  And find myself wondering why,

Why do they not scream out
  And grapple star against star,
Seeking for blood in the wood,
  As all things round me are?

One might take this for a rather superficial reflection on the general viciousness of the world, but Dunsany had something specific in mind. In *Patches of Sunlight* he explains that he wrote the poem during the First World War, "under the stimulus of shellfire." During a barrage he looked at the night sky and was impressed by the way the sky seemed so peaceful when shells were landing all around and men were dying on the ground. With a little imagination the scene can be visualized: Dunsany huddled in a trench in the mud and the dark, the constant flashes of the shellbursts becoming almost a steady, lurid glow, perhaps wounded men crying out nearby, and the barren ruin of No Man's Land stretched out before him. Overhead, the sky is clear and filled with bright stars. But there's none of that actually *in* the poem. There is no intensity of feeling, or even anything sufficiently concrete to let the reader know what he's talking about. This is why Dunsany's verse is so inferior to his prose. It presents not a vivid picture, but a thick fog.

Occasionally his poems could be witty. "Ode to a Dublin Critic" is an answer to prejudiced reviewers who not only

didn't like fantasy, but were sure all aristocrats were dil-
ettantes. There is a fill-in-the-blanks quality to the piece,
and sometimes it is awkward, but there are good lines:

> And lesser journalists have said,
>   That cannot see such things themselves,
> The man is clearly off his head
>   To write of things like gods and elves.

> By walls of cities not of Earth
>   All wild my winged dreams have run,
> And known the demons that had birth
>   In planets of another sun.

> From little fountain-pens they wring
>   The last wee drop of inky spite;
> "We do not like the kind of thing
>   "That lords," they say, "mostly write."

There is no need to go on like this. At best, Dunsany's
poetry is minor, usually light verse. At worst it is doggerel.
Fifty Poems is particularly tedious because virtually every
item in it has the same rhyme scheme; and one after another, they can put the reader to sleep. His other poetry
books are nearly as bad. He published five collections of
short verse and two book-length poems. These, *A Journey*
(about his trip to Greece during World War II) and *The
Year* (a diary in verse) are best endured a little bit at a time,
or better yet, not at all. His last collection, *To Awaken Pegasus* (1949) is somewhat better than the rest and deserves
consideration since it contains two or three poems worth

[131]

PATHWAYS TO ELFLAND

reading, including "Ulysses, Bound to the Mast," which Dunsany thought to be his best. By all indications it was. This is the first stanza:

> Turn landward! If I said a while ago
> "Heed not my orders," I was ignorant then.
> I had not heard this song, and could not know.
> I spoke at random. Heed me now, my men.
> Take out the wax I sealed your ears with then
> I played that jest on you, for 'twas no more.
> I brought you from the Cyclops' dreadful den.
> Turn landward: let us lie upon that shore
> While days like happy dreams drift by us
> evermore.

Homer, this isn't, but it is at least fairly readable. If the poem had been Dunsany's average instead of his best, he might have been an acceptable, if not very important poet. Unfortunately it wasn't. The collection still contains horrors, like "The Three Sisters:"

> For we are both among the ancient powers.
> I thought of Wilson and Canute, who tried
> To stop these things; then said "Some plan of ours
> May yet control you." "Control first the tide,"
> She said, "and, after that, abate my pride.
> I and the sea and thunder, what are we
> That man should curb us?" "Wait till they decide:
> There'll be some plan," I said. "All men agree
> That you must be controlled." A long laugh hooted
> she.

The above would have worked better in prose, in a short
fable like those in *Fifty-One Tales*. Then it might have been
only mediocre.

The only conclusion is that Dunsany possessed little talent for this kind of verse. Anyone who could write as many
poems as he did, and still write badly at the end, probably
couldn't do any better. But he was unable to see this because
of his distrust for criticism (He wrote, "Criticism is like
giving Latin names to dead butterflies, while fancy is like
a live butterfly on the wind.") and his rigidly conservative
ideas about what poetry should be.

He was very much behind the times, although in art that
isn't always a fault. He thought poetry should express
beauty and exhort men to virtue. Hazel Littlefield Smith,
in her *Lord Dunsany: King of Dreams*, quotes him as saying
that the purpose of poetry is to "make clear the concept
of the moral responsibiltiy of mankind." Certainly medieval Christian poets would have agreed, as would Homer,
who was very interested in showing examples of virtue and
vice. But this sense of high seriousness and dogmatism
(which just as easily could have been "the purpose of poetry
is to incite the masses to revolution") is the very thing which
wrecked Dunsany. He failed precisely because he was unable to meet his own standards. He rarely presented beauty
nearly as effectively in verse as he did so often in his prose,
and his poems are not particularly morally uplifting. Had
he been willing to write flights of imaginative fancy in verse
similar to what *A Dreamer's Tales* was in prose and ignore
the moralism and edification, he might have gotten somewhere. Had he tried it, he might have had a talent for
nonsense verse.

PATHWAYS TO ELFLAND

But he wrote many times that poetry is a sacred calling and had the romantic notion that a Poet with a capital P is someone very special indeed. He concluded *Nowadays* thus:

For what is it to be a poet? It is to see at a glance the glory of the earth, to see beauty in all its forms and manifestations, to feel ugliness like a pain, to resent the wrongs of others as bitterly as one's own, to know mankind as others know single men, to know nature as botanists know a flower, to be thought a fool, to hear at times the clear voice of God.

What has that got to do with writing verse? Couldn't one do it just as well in prose? A poet may be a good poet or a bad one, which is mostly a matter of talent and mastery of technique, and he might be a good person or a scoundrel (e.g. François Villon), but the same is also true of any artist.

If Dunsany was a "poet" by his own definition, it is in his early short stories. *The Gods of Pegāna* borders on poetry as it stands, and passages from his stories, if rearranged typographically, might make better verse than his rhymed stuff. (This idea is hardly unique. A book of Thomas Wolfe's "poetry" was published that way, all of it pulled from his novels.) Consider these three paragraphs of "Where the Tides Ebb and Flow." Not a mark of punctuation has been changed, but now it is "verse":

The ebb came
And I saw the dead eyes of the houses

And the jealousy of other forgotten things
That storm had not carried thence.

And some more centuries passed over the ebb and flow
And over the loneliness of things forgotten.
And I lay there all the while
In the careless grip of the mud,
Never wholly covered,
Yet never able to go free,
And I longed for the great caress of the warm Earth
Or the comfortable lap of the Sea.

Of course such an idea is heresy; and while Dunsany became an innovator by tolerating a little heresy in prose, he couldn't in verse. Such a thing would have smacked of modernism, and his tastes were for the Elizabethans foremost and the early Romantics secondly. He disliked intellectual poetry, and considered the time between the death of Herrick and the beginning of Shelley's career "the dark century." This, however, was not nearly as dark as the 20th century, in his view. He detested that modern verse which deals with ugliness and that which is obscure. T.S. Eliot was singled out as a special villain, perhaps because everyone was proclaiming him a genius at the time and Dunsany thought this an insult to honest poets. An element of envy might also have been present; and, as Amory points out, this didn't do much for his reputation. Writers are seldom at their best tearing down other writers.

Dunsany owned copies of Eliot's works and scrawled acidic comments in the margins. He called the plays "frightful nonsense" and claimed that he had "brought poetry to the lowest ebb it has ever known," then went on to add, "I don't mean that he writes it, but that he has overthrown it." He accused Eliot of "ignorance of plain English and the inability to write clearly."

This rose to an obsession in Dunsany's last years, so for him to write free-form poetry would have been capitulation to the enemy. So he was stuck in a kind of verse which didn't suit his talent, and remained a third-rater. The judgment of subsequent generations has been against him, and his poetry remains forgotten, probably deservedly.

Non-Fiction

Dunsany's non-fiction is of secondary interest, but much of it is still worth reading. Foremost are his three volumes of autobiography, *Patches of Sunlight* (1938), *While The Sirens Slept* (1944), and *The Sirens Wake* (1945). Those who expect an author to reveal his innermost feelings in his autobiography will be disappointed, however. The most remarkable thing about these three books is how entertaining Dunsany could be without telling very much about himself. Of course this is because the books were written for publication (in fact, at the request of the publisher), and he was much too dignified to lay his psyche bare before an audience.

Patches of Sunlight is deliberately structured to be evasive. The title means that only the "sunny" parts of his life will be considered, the boring or unpleasant ones being best left hidden. Dunsany glosses over his childhood and youth, mentions his first trip abroad (to Switzerland, when he was 16), then goes on to his first literary experiences, scarcely touching on such personal things as his romance with Beatrice or their marriage. Always avoiding the limelight, even in a book supposedly about himself, he fills pages with amusing anecdotes about other people, descriptions of Egyptian ruins and African safaris, and the like. If he had ever been so inclined, he probably could have written first-rate travel books, but he explains that he is not so inclined because he doesn't regard such works as art. Art, he says, should preserve the simple beauties of nature or else create things which do not exist. Travel books do neither, nor do autobiographies, which, further, run the risk of garrulity, which is poor form.

Yet some of the best parts occur when he violates his own rules and writes about unpleasant things, such as the Easter Rebellion. He was on leave at the time and, always a staunch loyalist, rushed to Dublin to offer his services to the British as soon as hostilities broke out. A car in which he and a friend were riding came up against a barricade manned by rebels, who opened fire. Dunsany was hit in the face, and both of them captured. He was taken to a hospital and treated like a patient, not a prisoner. One of the nuns who was trying to go about her business complained about the "nasty little things" pinging against the windows—bullets. Later, when the combatants began to use artillery, a lot of glass was broken but the hospital wasn't hit. Meanwhile his friend wasn't being maltreated either. He was subsisting mostly on wines at the enemy headquarters, and when the Nationalists began to lose and became despondent, he asked to see their plan. They showed it to him and he said words to the effect of, "That's a terrible plan. You'd best surrender immediately." They did, and slightly tipsy, he brought in several hundred prisoners. *Up in the Hills* is almost believable in the light of

NON-FICTION

such accounts.

The First World War dominates much of the latter part of *Patches of Sunlight*, and again Dunsany has to talk about unhappy things or else skip the period entirely. He does not relate any first-hand horrors, but he does devote a few melancholy chapters to friends he has lost and the devastation he has seen in France.

Also, this volume contains more about Dunsany's writing than the other two. He cannot explain a flight of fancy, save to call it what it is, and thus can't tell the "source" for Pegāna, which is probably just as well. But he does put forth a wealth of information about his writing methods,* his artistic credo, his early experiences in the theatre, and his interests in literature.

While the Sirens Slept is more of the same, only less of it. The sirens of the title are air-raid sirens, by the way, not those which Odysseus heard, and thus the book covers the period in which these sirens were not singing—between the wars. It begins with Dunsany's first trip to America (a lecture tour, during which H.P. Lovecraft saw him and became interested in his works, surely a major event in the history of fantasy, if unbeknownst to Dunsany), then goes on with more travels, anecdotes, chess games (a matter-of-fact account of playing the world champion to a draw), and lots more about sport, complete with quotes from Dunsany's hunting diary. Some of this is interesting and

---

* One, which he doesn't bother to mention, but which Lady Dunsany related to Sprague de Camp, was that he always sat on a crumpled old hat while composing his tales. Perhaps it had magical properties; but, alas, some visitor to Dunsany Castle made off with it, so we'll never know.

some of it is not. The tallies of kills will seem positively obscene to many modern readers.

The highlight is the trip to India made in 1928. There, as a member of the aristocracy and with letters of introduction from other peers, Dunsany was able to stay with various Indian rulers. Thus he found himself in Oriental courts nearly as exotic as anything he imagined in his early stories.

He stayed a month with the Nawab of Rampur, during which time two incidents occurred which illustrated the basic goodness of Dunsany's character. He doesn't pat himself on the back when he relates them, but just includes them with everything else.

The first happened on a hunting expedition. His host knew how eager Dunsany was to bag a tiger and spared no expense putting together a safari. A forest fire broke out, and the party had to flee. Dunsany, as an honored guest, was given an especially swift elephant to escape on, but he refused it, unwilling to leave his guides behind to burn. Happily, all got away safely.

Some while later he, his son Randal, and one of the Nawab's sons were out driving. The ruler's son, who was at the wheel, tried to take a shortcut through the jungle and got stuck, leaving them unaccounted for overnight. At first the Nawab was worried and sent out motor patrols and a troop of cavalry to search. But when he found out what happened he was furious at his son, who was in a position, as Dunsany put it, akin to that of a British guard who had just dropped the crown jewels in the Thames and was trying to apologize. It seemed the unfortunate son would be in trouble for a long time, but it wasn't his fault, so Dunsany asked one favor of his host: that he forgive the young man.

He was visiting the Maharajah of Gwalior when he finally got his tiger. Dunsany was supposed to sit in the window of a tower while the tiger was driven by, and shoot it. But he thought it more sporting to meet the creature face-to-face, so before his guides could know what was happening, he went outside and shot the tiger as it came at him. He then turned around and was surprised to find that his gunbearer had been standing behind him all the time. The best he could make out, language being something of a problem, was that the man had wanted to be with him. Dunsany treated the people of the countries he visited with respect, as equals, and they respected him too.

Such episodes make it more plausible that the narrator of *Dean Spanley* conveniently knew a Maharajah who supplied him with the rare wine; all the ones Dunsany knew were that generous.

The Sirens Wake mostly covers the years of World War II. There are more hunting scores, visits to lords and ladies, and anecdotes; but less is said about Dunsany's writing except for increasingly frequent quotations from his poetry. This is the least interesting of the autobiographies, but it has its moments, most of them dealing with the Blitz and a trip to Greece in 1940. Incredibly, at the moment when England seemed about to lose the war, Dunsany was asked to fill the Byron Chair of English Literature at the University of Athens. To avoid U-boats, a round-about route was taken, by way of Glasgow and Capetown, followed by a leisurely flight the length of Africa. There is a vivid description of Abu Simbel seen from the air. After a brief stopover in Egypt, he went to Turkey, then to Greece, but a few months later Greece was invaded and Dunsany and his wife had to flee. He boarded a ship filled with refugees, wearing two hats because he didn't see why he should leave one behind for the Germans. During the voyage a Stuka tried to bomb the ship, but it was shot down and crashed into the sea. "Of his bones are coral made," wrote Dunsany of the pilot.

The book ends with his safe return to England, and he wrote no more about himself afterwards.

In 1943 he delivered lectures at Trinity College in Dublin on the arts of poetry, prose, and drama, which were later collected into a book called *The Donnellan Lectures* (1945). Dunsany was never much of a critic, but his ideas on drama were the best developed, as he had shown earlier in "The Carving of the Ivory." Hence, the lecture on drama is the best, and contains some genuinely practical advice. The one on poetry is filled with rhetoric and abstractions, and the one on prose is somewhat better, mostly preoccupied with correctness of language, the modern degeneration of English, and the importance of rhythm. He cited the King James version of *Ecclesiastes* as the high-water mark of English prose.

His other non-fiction books were *If I Were Dictator (The Pronouncements of the Fraud Macaroni)* (1934) and *My Ireland* (1937). The former is part of a series of books by various authors, all telling what they would do as dictator of England. Of course it was written to order, and Dunsany rarely did his best that way, but still he managed to be amusing, and even insightful on occasion. Despite the title, it has little to do with Mussolini, and is almost non-political. Dunsany spends most of his time outlawing such dire crimes as cutting dogs' tails and putting chalk in bread for whiteness, not to mention growing hedges too high for horses and hounds to get through. Probably his most useful proposal was the office of Verbal Incinerator, the holder of which was charged with eliminating those phrases in political speeches designed to confuse. He also warned printers that any commas dropped from Macaroni's pronouncements would be regarded as stolen state property.

My Ireland was something his agent arranged for him to do. It is allegedly about Ireland and its people, but it reads more like one of his autobiographies, only without any chronological sequence. He writes about the Irish countryside, extolling the beauties of undisturbed bogs. A chapter is devoted to Francis Ledwidge, a poet whose career Dunsany helped launch, but who was killed in the First World War. Ledwidge is the dead friend about whom "The Road" (in *Tales of War*) was written. There is another chapter about A.E. (George Russell), another poet who is better remembered today.

We are teased with politics. The big question at the time was what the Irish people thought about the new Republican Government. To get an answer to this, Dunsany tells us, one must ask a typical Irishman, and since a typical citizen of any country is an abstraction, he choses to interview a fictional character. He tells of a conversation with Old Mickey from *Up in the Hills*. The subject of the government comes up, but the two quickly agree it's not best to talk about politics. (True, considering what had been going on in Ireland for the previous 20 years.) This is an

[143]

amusing conceit, but when Dunsany uses it again a few chapters later, it is considerably less so. The book as a whole is extremely uneven, seemingly thrown together with little planning or effort. Nevertheless, when Methuen issued it in their "My Country" series, it sold well and went through several printings.

Finally, Dunsany's non-fictional works consist of various short articles. *A Glimpse from a Watchtower* is a completely unexceptional political pamphlet published in 1945. Various other articles are collected in *The Ghosts of the Heaviside Layer.* "Nowadays" and "The Fantastic Dreams" have already been discussed. "Decay in the Language" is about sloppy usage, redundant phrases like "weather conditions" and nouns used as adjectives ("The mystery man in the luxury car"), among other things. Some of his arguments have dated badly. We just don't write "to-day" with a hyphen anymore. "The Authorship of *Barrack-Room Ballads*" is a very funny piece "proving" that Swinburne *didn't* write Kipling, in the way some people "prove" Bacon wrote Shakespeare. There are also several nature articles, a tribute to Sime, a discussion of aristocracy ("A Word for Fallen Grandeur") and even something on Dunsany's hobby of carving clay figures.

One of his favorite topics was writers he had known. "Four Poets," which was perhaps the last thing submitted to an editor during his lifetime (it was published shortly after his death), is a collection of reminiscences about A.E., Kipling, Yeats, and James Stephens. To the very end he was telling amusing anecdotes:

> Many writers have poses. Shaw's pose, for instance,

was that of a gruff man writing unfriendly post cards; but as I saw him he was the opposite of that, and I always saw him friendly and kind. But Yeats's whole life was a pose, a bubble often mischievously pricked by the rather naughty pin of Oliver Gogharty, as when, with probably more wit than accuracy, he went around Dublin saying, "Yeats has been evicting imaginary tenants in County Kildare." [Yeats always wanted to be a landed aristocrat.]

Uncollected Works

As this book was going to press, the author, in collaboration with the noted Lovecraft scholar, S.T. Joshi, began work on what we hope to be the definitive bibliography of Dunsany's work, listing all books in every edition and variant; book appearances of shorter work; and periodical publications, both originals and reprints. In the course of researching the periodicals, so much more previously unknown, uncollected material was discovered that it became necessary to, in the alleged parlance of newspapermen, stop the presses.

The present count stands at seventy short stories and forty-six essays, although in some cases the difference between a story and an essay is so slight that it becomes a judgement call, and the piece might be better described as an imaginative sketch. The material comes from every period of Dunsany's career, and in some cases reveals wholly unsuspected aspects of his literary activity.

He was a regular contributor to *The Saturday Review* of England before World War I. In *The Book of Wonder* there is a notice acknowledging that all the stories had previously appeared in *The Saturday Review*. Further, many of the tales from the other early collections appeared there, some under different titles. "Where the Tides Ebb and Flow" first saw light far less impressively as "The Terrible Dream."

But among these familiar stories are many unreprinted items. There are short allegories which could easily have been included in *Fifty-One Tales*. For example, "The Eight Wishes" tells how Satan gets God's permission to grant man seven wishes. Man asks for cities, weapons, etc., and creates modern civilization. When man asks for an eighth wish, to set the world back the way it was, God refuses. "How Care Would Have Dealt with the Nomads" presents typically romanticized Arabs. Hurry and Care cannot vex them, because they can't find the nomads in the vast expanse of the desert.

Some of these little fables were perhaps left unreprinted because of topicality. "Our Laurels," published in the early months of World War I, tells how a poet's laurels won't grow. But in wartime they do and become immortal. War inspires great art. "Exchange No Robbery" is a veiled attack on someone: In a far land, poets are honored. In ours, ruffians (who cause social discontent) are. A poet from our world and a ruffian from the other change places. The author refuses to identify the honored ruffian, but implies it is a specific person. This was published in 1912, so the obvious target of the Kaiser seems less likely.

The most datedly obscure of all is "A Cricket Match" (1912), a political satire about a match between then current British politicians. Adding to the difficulty is the game of cricket itself, the fine details and nuances of which remain forever incomprehensible to Americans.

[147]

PATHWAYS TO ELFLAND

The very best of the fiction or near-fiction from *The Saturday Review* are two sketches, "Romance" and "Jetsam," both of which date from about the same time as the stories in *A Dreamer's Tales*. The first tells of the revelations of the allegorical figure of Romance and how he is always banished by Time, and the second is about the debris left behind by the years. (Time is compared to an ocean.) Both are very beautiful, not quite unified or structured enough to be considered stories. They make an interesting comparison to "Blagdaross" (in *A Dreamer's Tales*), which is right on the frontier of the short story, the prose poem, and the imaginative essay.

Dunsany also contributed reviews of plays and occasional books to *The Saturday Review*. As a critic he tended to be long on description and short on analysis, and he wrote in a lusher, more poetic manner than is typical for criticism, but in the hindsight of nearly seventy years he is on the right side more often than not. He is at his best praising Synge's *Deirdre of the Sorrows;* but, to a reader of the 1980s, perhaps going too far when he proclaims *The Blue Bird* a tremendous masterpiece. His comparison of Maeterlink to Vergil seems very strange.

There was a sudden flurry of publications in American magazines in 1919, around the time of Dunsany's first American tour. One gets the impression from editorial comments that he brought a bundle of manuscripts with him, and handed them out to the editors he met. The bibliographer discovers that he may have handed the *same* manuscript to more than one editor.

Several stories appeared in *Vanity Fair,* including some of those in *Tales of Three Hemispheres*, and a few uncollected ones. Very much in the familiar manner is "The Golden City of Joy," in which every attempt to build such a city fails. The city keeps sinking into the earth. But a grim man builds a grim city on the hard mud of War; and this, seen in the sunset and distance, becomes the City of Joy. The message is obvious, but the piece is no weaker as a story than many of the lesser items in *Three Hemispheres*.

"Two Sketches" is allegory of a different sort, more directly political than most of the reprinted works. In the first sketch, which is told in an Irish brogue, Saint Patrick is busily clearing Ireland of snakes when he meets Satan, who challenges him to a coin-flip. If the saint wins, he can drive out the snakes. If the Devil wins, he gets to create something far worse to plague the Irish. The Devil cheats, and wins, and creates agitators. In the second sketch, the Unicorn guards the Shield alone, for the Lion is dead. Then the Shield is gone, but the Unicorn guards its memory. The reference is obviously to the British coat of arms. Dunsany the Loyalist is taking a contrary view of the then-current strife which the Irish later came to call their War of Independence.

The other major concentration of uncollected pieces is in the British humor magazine *Punch*, in issues dating from the middle 1930s into the early '50s. Most of these appeared anonymously, or signed only with an initial, but all are identified in the *Punch* index. And to read them is to recognize them. The bulk of them, taken together, reveals Dunsany as a topical humorist rather like James Thurber, Robert Benchley, or Art Buchwald. While some of the pieces are full and complete stories, they tend to be anecdotes or just imaginary conversations outlining an amusing

[149]

PATHWAYS TO ELFLAND

(sometimes political) idea. Here we have more the Dunsany of *If I Were Dictator* than of his famous fiction.

The work from the World War II era is the least interesting, perhaps for the same reason that Charlie Chaplin's *The Great Dictator*, while respected, is hardly the most widely-shown of his films. Making fun of Hitler doesn't seem funny anymore, in light of post-war revelations. But in January 1940, it was still amusing to suggest that the German dictator was misunderstood: he is an honest man, but for security reasons he is impersonated by thousands of look-alikes, who aren't. A few months earlier, Dunsany had proposed demilitarizing Hitler's moustache. Perhaps the one item in this group which still works is "Into the Consommé" (September 11, 1940): A man finds a fly in his soup. He fishes it out, but it crawls back in, again and again. It must be a reincarnated French politician, a fellow diner remarks.

The best *Punch* stories tend to be the more fully developed. Some are fantasy, but many are not. They are exaggerations and tall tales, often touching on fantastic matters, but only in the sense that the narrator is stretching things that much further.

Many are about the Irish peasantry and may be taken as examples of what tour guides call the Irish art of blarney. (Dunsany never used the term.) For example, in "A Let-Off," we read how the Irish were going to invade England circa 1920. But the Irish general saw two bad omens: a crowing hen and a red-haired woman on a bicycle. That woman never knew that she had saved London. Similarly, in the epic conflict of "The Battle of Killahoo," two Irishmen set to topping one another with such fine and mighty oaths that they forget what they're fighting about. In "The Rations of Murdoch Finucan," a policeman wants to ask this distinguished gentleman about his ration card. But Murdoch has been dead these three hundred years; and surely, the farmer who lives in his house says, the policeman doesn't want to face the wrathful ghost to begrudge him a cup of tea. The policeman can't. The implication, of course, is that the farmer made it all up. This is the familiar situation of the crafty peasant fooling the city person with a wild tale. It bears some resemblance to "A Royal Swan" (in *The Ghosts of the Heaviside Layer*).

A few of the stories are outright fantasies. "A Day on the Bog" involves two men and a leprechaun, who asks Mr. Fitzgerald, the most generous man in all Ireland, to lend him his soul. Mr. Fitzgerald will oblige; but, alas, he is a Protestant, so his soul won't do.

More overtly satirical is "A Modern Portrait," in which the narrator discovers that a seemingly surrealist portrait is in truth quite accurate. The mother of the woman who sat for it was a Victorian lady; the father, a bicycle.

Several of the *Punch* essays are amusing. "The Cipher" tells of a scholar who proves that the works of Shakespeare were written, not by Bacon, but by an obscure Elizabethan writer. Unfortunately the same cipher proves that the scholar's monumental treatise on this subject was really written by his rival. "Advance Regulations" gives the passenger rules for a train which runs through the Earth's core. "The Revenge," which—like "The Cipher"—is written in the form of a case-history rather than a story, tells of autograph collector who was the bane of all authors. He wrote them long and interesting letters which they had to

[151]

PATHWAYS TO ELFLAND

answer, and wasted a lot of their time. But then the collector becomes an author himself and the other authors get their revenge—and rich—by selling *his* letters.

In addition to *The Saturday Review* and *Punch* material, there is a wide miscellany of items from *The Spectator, The Strand, Time and Tide,* and other British and American magazines ranging from *John O'London's Weekly* to *Good Housekeeping*—far more than can be described in a single chapter.

Two stories particularly deserve notice, both because of their quality, and because they belong to that odd period in Dunsany's career (middle 1940s, around the time of the essay, "The Fantastic Dreams") in which he seemed to disown fantasy, and write of fantastic things only as lies or quaint delusions.

"The Story of Tse Gah" (*Tomorrow,* December 1947) is about a small boy in a Himalayan country who is taken to be the latest incarnation of a god. So he is dragged away by the priests and lives a miserable life, while they exploit his "prophecies." Then there is a revolution. All the priests are killed, and the boy, whose perceptions of reality have been badly skewed, tries to call down the thunder on the rebels. But nothing happens. The story has vastly more potential than Dunsany managed to realize. One wishes it could have been a fantasy, or else a more penetrating psychological study; but for all its abruptness and superficiality, it has an emotional quality which most late Dunsany lacks, and is strangely moving.

"Helping the Fairies" (*The Strand,* June 1947) is another Irish peasant story. This time an English farmer, living in

Ireland, has the nerve to cut down a thorn tree, sacred to the fairies. The locals predict that terrible luck will come on him as a result. But his luck continues to be unforgivably good, almost miraculous. This cannot be tolerated. It mocks the Irish, and even implies that the fairies don't exist. Finally, the peasants kill the Englishman, in order to "help" the fairies protect their reputation. "Helping the Fairies" is strikingly nastier than the usual "delusion" story. It makes an interesting contrast to the more gentle novella "The Man Who Ate the Phoenix."

From the mass of this material, we may conclude that Dunsany was a good editor of his own work. The stories he left out of his collections tended to be the weaker ones, or the more topical ones, which would date. Also, many of the political pieces might have offended, or even gotten him into trouble in Ireland after that country won its independence in the early '20s.

But the uncollected stories and essays include a great many which are worth reprinting. Some of the stories, we must assume, were just left out of his books for want of room. Others, perhaps, were too atypical of what readers expected from him. Much of the *Punch* material, right on the borderline between story and sketch, just didn't fit in anywhere.

There never was a general collection of Dunsany's essays, which explains why most of his short nonfiction is uncollected. Also, many of the polemical pieces repeat themselves. There are too many tirades on pet peeves: the cruelty of cutting dogs' tails, the decline in the standards of English usage, the evils of advertizing. At least four of these previously uncollected essays virtually repeat the contents of "Decay in the Language," which is collected in *The Ghosts of the Heaviside Layer*.

After World War II, Dunsany apparently experienced a great burst of creativity. As much as half of this material appeared in the middle to late '40s. But by that point, his popularity was waning. His books had ceased to appear in America, with the exception of *The Fourth Book of Jorkens*. The only later collections other than the last two Jorkens books were *The Man Who Ate the Phoenix* and *Little Tales of Smethers*. Anything that didn't fit into these didn't get reprinted.

Owlswick Press will publish a sequel to *The Ghosts of the Heaviside Layer*, containing a generous selection of this hitherto unknown Dunsany. There is much that is interesting among it, a good deal that is amusing, and even a few gems.

Conclusion

ime has treated Dunsany better than many other writers. He hovered on the edge of oblivion for a while, but never quite disappeared, and in recent years has undergone a considerable revival. Virtually all the early short stories have been reprinted in paperback within the last decade, and the Dover collection, *Gods, Men, and Ghosts,* may not sell widely, but it remains in print, making a selection of the best material readily available. Some of the early collections have been reprinted in facsimile by Books for Libraries Press and in completely new editions by Owlswick Press. Of the novels, *The Curse of the Wise Woman* and *My Talks With Dean Spanley* have seen recent hardcover printings, and *Don Rodriguez, The Charwoman's Shadow,* and *The King of Elfland's Daughter* have appeared in paperback. All the plays and all the poetry collections are out of print, as are the Jorkens books, *Little Tales of Smethers,* and *The Man Who Ate The Phoenix,* although one can hope the revival lasts long enough to get them reprinted. It would be nice to see new editions of the memoirs, but this isn't likely.

Dunsany's greatest virtues were an incredibly fertile

imagination and a stylistic mastery well beyond the ordinary. Nothing quite like his early stories exists in English, so they will always be assured some readership among those able to appreciate such things. The sort of reader who skims for content rather than actually reading the prose will be lost in them, but this is always the case. Survival and popularity are not the same thing. As long as any run-of-the-mill writer of the next generation *can* reproduce what a given author does, one *will*; and that past author will be forgotten: but if no one else can do it, as long as there is interest in that type of story, readers must go back to the original. Therefore Dunsany's work should survive as long as there is a readership for fantasy, which should be a long time. The fantastic represents a basic human mood, which has been with us since the beginning of literature, and it isn't likely to go away quickly, even if it may fall into the background for a while on occasion, as it did in the 1940s and '50s.

The essence of a Dunsany story is the language, the actual telling. Imagine a ballad sung by a singer with a beautiful voice, and again by someone who croaks like a frog. Both are telling the same story, but there is a world of difference. Imagine "The Fortress Unvanquishable Save for Sacnoth" written by James Fenimore Cooper, and if you don't get sick (or even if you do), the point becomes obvious.

What Dunsany lacked was emotional depth. In *The Gods of Pegāna* this hardly mattered, but in some of his later works it did. This is why many of them seem weak or superficial. There is a certain refusal to commit himself all the way, which is why *Guerilla* isn't as good as *The Red Badge*

CONCLUSION

of Courage, even though Dunsany had fought in two wars and Crane in none. He put himself into his work, but not very much of himself. Certainly anyone who could write three charming volumes of autobiography and say little about his feelings is at the very least a private man. Only *The Curse of the Wise Woman* has any personal intensity.

Of course it didn't do Dunsany much good, in terms of his morale and his career, to have written his most important work first. Had he written the "Wonder" books in the 1950s, they would have seemed the brilliant climax of an always interesting career. But as it happened, one could say, "Lord Dunsany? Yes, he did his best work back before the First World War. Not quite what he used to be, I'm afraid."

In the very long run, after an author and his critics are dead, when one has to read books like this one to find out what was written when, none of this matters. The good work survives out of context with the rest.

Dunsany was not a *great* writer in the sense of being one of the most towering figures in all of world literature. He was not one of the influential thinkers of the 20th century. He was a great fantasist. His work is entertaining, and much of it is beautiful; and that is enough. A sculptor who does little statues with consummate skill is producing something perfectly valid, even if it is not on the same scale as a carving wrought out of the side of a mountain.

One needs a sense of perspective in these things, and this sense tells us that there will be other important fantasy writers in the future, but there will never be another Lord Dunsany.

Appendix

Note: Main sources of information for this chronology of the plays were Dunsany's three volumes of autobiography. He kept lists of when his works were written, and refers to them often. Other sources were Bierstadt's *Dunsany the Dramatist*, Amory's *Lord Dunsany: A Biography*, Smith's *Lord Dunsany: King of Dreams*, the collected theatre reviews from *The New York Times*, and various indexes of reviews, drama in periodicals, etc. Question marks indicate doubtful cases. Dashes mean that the play in question almost certainly was never performed or published.

Plays by Lord Dunsany

TITLE	WRITTEN	PRODUCED	PUBLISHED
The Glittering Gate (1 act)	March 23, 1909	*Dublin*, Abbey Theatre, April 29, 1909	*Five Plays*, 1914
King Argimenes and the Unknown Warrior (2 acts)	Feb. 22–23, 1910	*Dublin*, Abbey Theatre, Jan. 26, 1911 *London*, Court Theatre, 1912 *New York.* Portmanteau Theatre, Dec. 18, 1916 Sept. 1911	*Five Plays*, 1914
The Gods of the Mountain (3 acts)	Summer 1910	*London*, Haymarket	*The Irish Review*, Dec. 1911

		Theatre, June 1, 1911 *Buffalo, NY*, Teck Theatre, April 8, 1912 *New York*, Shubert Theatre, April 11, 1912	*Five Plays*, 1914
The Murderers (1 act)	June 6, 1910	*New Haven, Ct*, Yale Univ., 1919	——
The Golden Doom (1 act)	Aug. 19–21, 1910	*London*Haymarket Theatre Nov. 19, 1912 *Poetry and Drama* #1, Dec., 1913 *Hartford, CT*, Portmanteau Theatre, Oct. 24, 1916	*Five Plays*, 1914
The Tents of the Arabs (2 acts)	Sept 3 & 8, 1910	*Paris*, Le Petit Theatre Anglais, Apr. 1914 *Detroit*, Arts and Crafts Theatre, Nov. 1916	*Smart Set*, March 1915 *Plays of Gods and Men*, 1917
The Lost Silk Hat (1 act)	Nov. 10, 1912	*Manchester*, The Gaiety Theatre, Aug. 4, 1913	*Five Plays*, 1914
The Laughter of Gods (3 acts)	Jan. 29, Feb. 2–3, 1911	*New York*, Portmanteau Theatre, Jan, 1919 *Prague*, State Theater, 1920	*Plays of Gods and Men*, 1917
A Night at the Inn (1 act)	Jan. 17, 1912	*New York*, Neighborhood Playhouse, Nov. 14, 1916	Sunwise Turn, Inc., 1916 (separate publication) *Plays of Gods and Men, 1917*
Alexander (4 acts)	April–July 1912	*Malvern* (England) Festival, 1938	*Alexander and Three Small Plays*, 1926

PATHWAYS TO ELFLAND

The Ginger Cat (3 acts)	Oct. 2–6 and 10–12, 1911	——	——
The Queen's Enemies (1 act)	Apr. 1913	New York, The Neighborhood Playhouse, Nov. 14, 1916	Plays of Gods and Men, 1917
Cheezo (1 act)	Spring 1917	?	Plays of Near and Far, 1922
The Old King's Tale (1 act)	Spring 1917	?	Alexander and Three Small Plays
Fame and the Poet (1 act)	Spring 1917	Cambridge, MA, Harvard Univ., 1919 St. Louis, Fall 1919	Atlantic, Aug. 1919 Plays of Near and Far, 1922
The Old Folk of the Centuries (3 acts)	Dec. 1918	?	1930
The Prince of Stamboul(1 act)	1918	?	Harper's Bazaar (?) Webber & Webster, ed. Short Plays for Junior and Senior Highschools, Houghton Mifflin, 1925 The Ghosts of The Heaviside Layer, 1980
The Compromise of the King of the Golden Isles (1 act)	?	New Haven, CT, Yale Univ., 1919	Plays of Near and Far, 1922
A Good Bargain (1 act)	Fall 1919	St. Louis, The Artists' Guild, 1920	The Smart Set, Dec. 1920 Plays of Near and Far, 1922
If (4 acts)	1919	London, Ambassador Theatre, May 1921 New York, The Little Theatre, Oct. 25, 1927	1921

[160]

APPENDIX

The Flight of the Queen (1 act)	July 1920	?	*Plays of Near and Far*, 1922
If Shakespeare Had Lived Today (1 act)	?	?	*Atlantic*, Oct. 1920 *Plays of Near and Far*, 1922
Mr. Faithful (3 acts)	May 1922	*London*, Lyric Hammersmith Theatre, 1922 (?) *BBC* radio (short version) 1930s (?)	1935
Lord Adrian (3 acts)	Oct. 1922, April 1923	*Hull* (England), 1923 *Dublin*, The Gate Theatre, April 16, 1937	1933 *The Ghosts of The Heaviside Layer*, 1980
The Jest of Hahalaba (1 act)	1926	?	*Atlantic*, Jan. 1927 *Seven Modern Comedies*, 1928
The Raffle (1 act)	July 5, 1926	?	*Seven Modern Comedies*, 1928
Atalanta at Wimbledon (1 act)	Aug. 19, 1927	?	*Seven Modern Comedies*, 1928
The Journey of the Soul (1 act)	?	?	*Seven Modern Comedies*, 1928
In Holy Russia (1 act)	?	?	*Seven Modern Comedies*, 1928
His Sainted Grandmother (1 act)	?	?	*Seven Modern Comedies*, 1928
The Hopeless Passion of Mr. Bunyon (1 act)	?	?	*Seven Modern Comedies*, 1928
The Evil Kettle (1 act)	?	?	*Alexander and Three Small Plays*, 1926

PATHWAYS TO ELFLAND

The Amusements of Khan Karuda (1 act)	?	?	*Alexander and Three Small Plays*, 1926
The Strange Lover (length?)	mid-1930s (?)	*Dublin*, The Players of Dublin, 1938	——
Fame Comes Late (1 act)	1933	?	*Plays for Earth and Air*, 1937
A Matter of Honor (1 act)	?	?	*Plays for Earth and Air*, 1937
Mr. Sliggens's Hour (1 act)	?	?	*Plays for Earth and Air*, 1937
The Pumpkin (1 act)	?	?	*London Mercury*, June 1931 *Plays for Earth and Air*, 1937
The Use of Man (1 act)	?	*BBC* radio, 1930s	*Plays for Earth and Air*, 1937
The Bureau de Change (1 act)	?	*BBC* radio, 1930s	*Plays for Earth and Air*, 1937
The Golden Dragon City (1 act)	?	*BBC* radio, 1930s	*Plays for Earth and Air*, 1937
The Seventh Symphony (1 act)	?	*BBC* radio, 1930s	*Plays for Earth and Air*, 1937
Time's Joke (1 act)	?	*BBC* radio, 1930s	*Plays for Earth and Air*, 1937
Atmospherics (1 act)	?	*BBC* radio, 1930s	*Plays for Earth and Air*, 1937
The Road (length?)	early 1950s	*Shoreham*, The Shoreham Players, early 1950s	——
Power (fragment)	circa 1954	——	——

Bibliography

Books By Lord Dunsany

1. *The Gods of Pegāna*. London: Elkin Matthews, 1905. Story Collection: The Gods of Pegāna. Of Skarl the Drummer. Of the Making of the Worlds. Of the Game of the Gods. The Chaunt of the Gods. The Sayings of Kib. Concerning Sish. The Sayings of Slid. The Deeds of Mung. The Chaunt of the Priests. The Sayings of Limpang-Tung. Of Yoharneth-Lahai. Of Roon the God of Going. The Revolt of the Home Gods. Of Dorozhand. The Eye in the Waste. Of the Thing That Is Neither God Nor Beast. Yonath the Prophet. Yug the Prophet. Alhireth-Hotep the Prophet. Kabok the Prophet. Of the Calamity That Befell Yūn-Ilāra by the Sea, and of the Building of the Tower of the Ending of Days. Of How the Gods Whelmed Sidith. Of How Imbaun Met Zodrak. Pegāna. The Sayings of Imbaun. Of How Imbaun Spake of Death to the King. Of Ood. The River. The Bird of Doom and the End.

2. *Time and the Gods*. London: Heinemann, 1906. Story collection: Time and the Gods. The Coming of the Sea. A Legend of the Dawn. The Vengeance of Men. When the Gods Slept. The King That Was Not. The Cave of Kai. The Sorrow of the Search. The Men of Yarnith. For the Honor of the Gods. Night and Morning. Usury. Mlideen. The Secret of the Gods. The South Wind. In the Land of Time. The Relenting of Sarnidac. The Jest of the Gods. The Dreams of the Prophet. The Journey of the King.

3. *The Sword of Welleran*. London: George Allen & Sons, 1908. Story

PATHWAYS TO ELFLAND

collection:
The Sword of Welleran. The Fall of Babbuklund. The Kith of the Elf-Folk. The Highwayman. In the Twilight. The Ghosts. The Whirlpool. The Hurricane. The Fortress Unvanquishable, Save for Sacnoth. The Lord of Cities. The Doom of La Traviata. On the Dry Land.

4. *A Dreamer's Tales*. London: George Allen & Sons, 1910. Story collection: Note: The Modern Library edition under this title also contains *The Sword of Welleran*.
Poltarnees, Beholder of Ocean. Blagdaross. The Madness of Andelsprutz. Where the Tides Ebb and Flow. Bethmoora. Idle Days on the Yann. The Sword and the Idol. The Idle City. The Hashish Man. Poor Old Bill. The Beggars. Carcassonne. In Zaccarath. The Field. The Day of the Poll. The Unhappy Body.

5. *The Book of Wonder*. London: Heinemann, 1912. Story collection: Note: The Modern Library edition under this title also contains *Time and the Gods*.
The Bride of the Man-Horse. The Distressing Tale of Thangobrind the Jeweller. The House of the Sphinx. The Probable Adventure of the Three Literary Men. The Injudicious Prayers of Pombo the Idolater. The Loot of Bombasharna. Miss Cubbidge and the Dragon of Romance. The Quest of the Queen's Tears. The Hoard of the Gibbelins. How Nuth Would Have Practised His Art Upon the Gnoles. How One Came, as was Foretold, to the City of Never. The Coronation of Mr. Thomas Shap. Chu-Bu and Sheemish. The Wonderful Window.

6. *Five Plays*, edited by Edwin Björkman. London: Grant Richards, 1914. Play collection:
The Gods of the Mountain. The Golden Doom. King Argimenes and the Unknown Warrior. The Glittering Gate. The Lost Silk Hat.

7. *Fifty-One Tales*. London: Elkin Matthews, 1915. Story collection:
The Assignation. Charon. The Death of Pan. The Sphinx at Gizeh. The Hen. Wind and Fog. The Raft-Builders. The Workman. The Guest. Death and Odysseus. Death and the Orange. The Prayer of the Flowers. Time and the Tradesman. The Little City. The Unpasturable Fields. The Worm and the Angel. The Songless City. The Latest Thing. The Demagogue and the Demi-Monde. The Giant Poppy. Roses. The Man with the Golden Ear-Rings. The Dream of King Karna-Vootra. The

BIBLIOGRAPHY

Storm. A Mistaken Identity. The True History of the Hare and the Tortoise. Alone the Immortals. A Moral Little Tale. The Return of Song. Spring in Town. How the Enemy Came to Thlumana. A Losing Game. Taking Up Piccadilly. After the Fire. The City. The Food of Death. The Lonely Idol. The Sphinx in Thebes (Massachusetts). The Reward. The Trouble in Leafy Green Street. The Mist. The Furrow-Maker. Lobster Salad. The Return of the Exiles. Nature and Time. The Song of the Blackbird. The Messengers. Three Tall Sons. Compromise. What We Have Come to. The Tomb of Pan.

8. *Tales of Wonder*. (American title: *The Last Book of Wonder*). London: Elkin Matthews, 1916. Story collection:
A Tale of London. Thirteen at Table. The City on Mallington Moor. Why the Milkman Shudders When He Perceives the Dawn. The Bad Old Woman in Black. The Bird of the Difficult Eye. The Long Porter's Tale. The Loot of Loma. The Secret of the Sea. How Ali Came to the Black Country. The Bureau d'Echange De Maux. A Story of Land and Sea. A Tale of the Equator. A Narrow Escape. The Watch-Tower. How Plash-Goo Came to the Land of None's Desire. The Three Sailors' Gambit. The Exiles' Club. The Three Infernal Jokes.

9. *Plays of Gods and Men*. Dublin: The Talbot Press, 1917. Play collection:
The Tents of the Arabs. The Laughter of the Gods. The Queen's Enemies. A Night at the Inn.

10. *Tales of War*. London: Elkin Matthews, 1918. Stories and sketches:
The Prayer of the Men of Daleswood. The Road. An Imperial Monument. A Walk to the Trenches. A Walk in Picardy. What Happened on the Night of the Twenty-Seventh. Standing To. The Splendid Traveller. England. Shells. Two Degrees of Envy. The Master of No Man's Land. Weeds and Wire. Spring in England and Flanders. The Nightmare Countries. Spring and the Kaiser. Two Songs. The Punishment. The English Spirit. An Investigation into the Causes and Origin of the War. Lost. The Last Mirage. A Famous Man. The Oases of Death. The Anglo-Saxon Tyranny. Memories. The Movement. Nature's Cad. The Home of Herr Schnitzelhaaser. A Deed of Mercy. The Last Scene of All. Old England.

11. *Nowadays*. Boston: The Four Seas Company, 1918. Speech on poetry.

[165]

PATHWAYS TO ELFLAND

12. *Unhappy Far-Off Things.* London: Elkin Matthews, 1919. World War I sketches:
A Dirge of Victory (verse). The Cathedral of Arras. A Good War. The House with Two Stories. Bermondsey Versus Wurtemburg. On an Old Battle Field. The Real Thing. A Garden of Arras. After Hell. A Happy Valley. In Bethune. In an Old Drawing-Room. The Homes of Arras.

13. *Tales of Three Hemispheres.* Boston: Luce & Company, 1919. Story collection. Note: the 1976 Owlswick edition contains an introduction by H.P. Lovecraft.
The Last Dream of Bwona Khubla. How the Office of Postman Fell Vacant in Otford-under-the-Wold. The Prayer of Boob Aheera. East and West. A Petty Quarrel. How the Gods Avenged Meuol Ki Ning. The Gifts of the Gods. A Sack of Emeralds. The Old Brown Coat. An Archive of the Older Mysteries. A City of Wonder. Idle Days on the Yann. A Shop in Go-By Street. The Avenger of Perdóndaris.

14. *If.* London: G.P. Putnam's Sons, 1921. Full-length play.

15. *The Chronicles of Rodriguez.* (American title: *Don Rodriguez: The Chronicles of Shadow Valley.*) London: G.P. Putnam's Sons, 1922. Novel.

16. *Plays of Near and Far.* London & New York: G.P. Putnam's Sons, 1922. Play collection: *Note*: the American edition contains a special preface.
The Compromise of the King of the Golden Isles. The Flight of the Queen. Cheezo. A Good Bargain. If Shakespeare Lived To-Day. Fame and the Poet.

17. *The King of Elfland's Daughter.* London & New York: G.P. Putnam's Sons, 1924. Novel.

18. *The Charwoman's Shadow.* London & New York: G.P. Putnam's Sons, 1926. Novel.

19. *Alexander and Three Small Plays.* London & New York: G.P. Putnam's Sons, 1925. Play collection:
Alexander. The Old King's Tale. The Amusements of Khan Kharuda. The Evil Kettle.

20. *The Blessing of Pan*. London & New York: G.P. Putnam's Sons, 1927. Novel.

21. *50 Poems*. London & New York: G.P. Putnam's Sons, 1929. Poetry collection.

22. *Seven Modern Comedies*. London & New York: G.P. Putnam's Sons, 1928. Play collection:
Atalanta at Wimbledon. The Raffle. The Journey of the Soul. In Holy Russia. His Sainted Grandmother. The Hopeless Passion of Mr. Bunyon. The Jest of Hahalaba.

23. *The Old Folk of the Centuries*. London: Elkin Matthews, 1930. Full-length play.

24. *The Travel Tales of Mr. Joseph Jorkens*. London & New York: G.P. Putnam's Sons, 1931. Story collection:
The Tale of the Abu Laheeb. The King of Sarahb. How Jembu Played for Cambridge. The Charm Against Thirst. Our Distant Cousins. A Large Diamond. A Queer Island. The Electric King. A Drink at a Running Stream. A Daughter of Ramses. The Showman. Mrs. Jorkens. The Witch of the Willows.

25. *Lord Adrian*. Waltham Saint Lawrence in Bershire: The Golden Cockerel Press, 1933. Full-length play.

26. *The Curse of the Wise Woman*. London: Heinemann, 1933. Novel.

27. *Jorkens Remembers Africa*. New York & Toronto: Longman's, Green, & Co., 1934. Story collection:
At the End of the Universe. An August in the Red Sea. Bare Truth. Black Mamba. The Club Secretary. The Correct Kit. The Curse of the Witch. Earth's Secret. Escape from the Valley. The Golden Gods. How Ryan Got Out of Russia. In the Garden of Memories. Lost Romance. A Mystery of the East. Ozymandias. The Pearly Beach. The Persian Spell. The Slugly Beast. Stranger than Fiction. A Walk to Lingham. What Jorkens Has to Put up with.

28. *If I Were Dictator: The Pronouncement of the Fraud Macaroni*. London: Methuen, 1934. Satirical essay.

PATHWAYS TO ELFLAND

29. *Mr. Faithful.* New York & London: Samuel French, 1935. Full-length play.

30. *My Talks With Dean Spanley.* London: Heinemann, 1936. Novel.

31. *Up in the Hills.* London: Heinemann, 1936. Novel.

32. *Rory and Bran.* London: Heinemann, 1936. Novel.

33. *My Ireland.* London: Jarrolds, 1937. Non-fiction.

34. *Plays for Earth and Air,* London: Heinemann, 1937. Play collection. Fame Comes Late. A Matter of Honor. Mr. Sliggens' Hour. The Pumpkin. The Use of Man. The Bureau d'Echange. The Golden Dragon City. The Seventh Symphony. Time's Joke. Atmospherics.

35. *Mirage Water.* London & New York: G.P. Putnam's Sons, 1938. Poetry collection.

36. *Patches of Sunlight.* London: Heinemann, 1938. Autobiography.

37. *The Story of Mona Sheehy.* London: Heinemann, 1939. Novel.

38. *War Poems.* London: Hutchison, 1940. Poetry collection.

39. *Jorkens Has a Large Whiskey.* London: G.P. Putnam's Sons, 1940. Story collection:
Jorkens' Revenge. Jorkens Retires from Business. Jorkens Handles a Big Property. The Invention of Dr. Caber. The Grecian Singer. The Jorkens Family Emeralds. A Fishing Story. Jorkens in High Finance. The Sign. The Angelic Shepherd. The Neopolitan Ice. The Development of the Rillswood Estate. The Fancy Man. The Lion and the Unicorn. A Doubtful Story. Jorkens Looks Forward. Jorkens Amongst the Ghosts. Elephant Shooting. African Magic. Jorkens Consults a Prophet. A Matter of Business. The Invention of the Age. The Sultan. The Monkey and the Banana. Pundleton's Audience. The Fight in the Drawing Room. The Ivory Poacher.

40. *Wandering Songs.* London: Hutchinson, 1943. Poetry collection.

BIBLIOGRAPHY

41. *The Journey*. London: MacDonald, 1944. Book-length poem.

42. *While the Sirens Slept*. London: Hutchinson, 1944. Autobiography.

43. *Guerilla*. London: Heinemann, 1944. Novel.

44. *The Sirens Wake*. London: Hutchinson, 1945. Autobiography.

45. *The Donnellan Lectures 1943*. London: Heinemann, 1945. Essay collection:
Prose. Poetry. Drama.

46. *The Year*. London: Jarrolds, 1946. Book-length poem.

47. *A Glimpse from a Watchtower*. London: Jarrolds, 1946 (pamphlet).
Collection of political essays.

48. *The Odes of Horace*, translated into English verse. London: Heinemann, 1947.

49. *The Man Who Ate the Phoenix*. London: Jarrolds, 1947. Story collection:
The Man Who Ate the Phoenix. The Widow Flynn's Apple Tree.
Where Everyone's Business is Known. The Rose By-Pass. An Old Man's
Tale. How the Tinker Came to Skavangur. The Opal Arrow-head. The
Sultan's Pet. The Present of the Sultan of Khash. The Policeman's
Prophecy. The Wind in the Wood. The Tiger's Skin. The Finding of
Mr. Jupkens. The Awful Dream. Mrs. Mulger. The Choice. Rose Tibbets. Little Snow White Up to Date. The Return. The Mad Ghost. The
Cause. The Cut. The Sleuthing of Lily Bostum. The Possibility of Life
on the Third Planet. Old Emma. How Abdul Din Saved Justice. The
First Watch-Dog. The Chess-Player, the Financier, and Another. The
Honorary Member. The Experiment. Down Among the Kingcups. The
Gratitude of the Devil. The After-dinner Speech. The Je-Ne-Sais-Quoi.
Poseidon. A Near Thing. Ardor Canis. A Lapse of Memory. Forty Years
On. The Iron Door. The Great Scoop.

50. *The Fourth Book of Jorkens*. London: Jarrolds, 1948. Story collection:
Making Fine Weather. Mgamu. The Haunting of Halahanstown. The
Pale-Green Image. Jorkens Leaves Prison. The Warning. The Sacred

PATHWAYS TO ELFLAND

City of Krakovlitz. Jorkens Practises Medicine and Magic. Jarton's Disease. On the Other Side of the Sun. The Rebuff. Jorkens' Ride. The Secret of the Sphinx. The Khamseen. The Expulsion. The Welcome. By Command of the Pharaoh. A Cricket Problem. A Life's Work. The Ingratiating Smile. The Last Bull. The Strange Drug of Dr. Caber. A Deal with the Devil. Strategy at the Billiards Club. Jorkens in the Witch Wood. Lost. The English Magnifico. The Cleverness of Dr. Caber. Fairy Gold. A Royal Dinner. A Fight with Knives. In a Dim Room.

51. *To Awaken Pegasus*. Oxford: G. Ronald, 1949. Poetry collection.

52. *The Strange Journeys of Colonel Polders*. London: Jarrolds, 1950. Novel.

53. *The Last Revolution*. London: Jarrolds, 1951. Novel.

54. *His Fellow Men*. London: Jarrolds, 1952. Novel.

55. *The Little Tales of Smethers*. London: Jarrolds, 1952. Story collection:
The Two Bottles of Relish. The Shooting of Constable Slugger. An Enemy of Scotland Yard. The Second Front. The Two Assassins. Kriegblut's Disguise. The Mug in the Gambling Hell. The Clue. Once Too Often. An Alleged Murder. The Waiter's Story. A Trade Dispute. The Pirate of the Round Pond. A Victim of Bad Luck. The New Master. A New Murder. A Tale of Revenge. The Speech. The Lost Scientist. The Unwritten Thriller. In Ravencore. Among the Bean Rows. The Death-Watch Beetle. Murder by Lightning. The Murder in Netherby Gardens. The Shield of Athene.

56. *Jorkens Borrows Another Whiskey*. London: Michael Joseph, 1954. Story collection:
The Two Way War. A Nice Lot of Diamonds. Letting Bygones be Bygones. The Lost Invention. On Other Paths. The Partner. Poulet à la Richelieu. A Walk in the Night. One Summer's Evening. A Friend of the Evening. An Eccentricity of Genius. Influenza. The Unrecorded Test Match. Idle Tears. Among the Neutrals. An Idyll of the Sahara. The Devil Among the Willows. A Spanish Castle. The New Moon. The Gods of Clay. A Rash Remark. The Story of Jorkens' Watch. The Track Through the Wood. Snow Water. The Greatest Invention. The Verdict. A Conversation in Bond Street. The Reward. Which Way? A Desperado in Surrey. Misadventure. A Long Memory. An Absentminded Profes-

sor. Greek Meets Greek.

57. *The Ghosts of the Heaviside Layer and Other Fantasms*, edited by Darrell Schweitzer. Philadelphia: Owlswick Press, 1980. Collection of stories, essays, plays:
The Ghosts of the Heaviside Layer. Told Under Oath. The Field Where the Satyrs Danced. By Night in the Forest. A Royal Swan. How the Lost Causes Were Removed from Valhalla. Correcting Nature. Autumn Cricket. In the Mojave. The Ghost of the Valley. The Ghost in the Old Corridor. Jorkens's Problem. The Revelation to Mr. Periple. A Fable for Moderns. The Fantastic Dreams. Nowadays. Ghosts. Irish Writers I Have Known. Four Poets. The Authorship of *Barrack Room Ballads*. Sime. Artist and Tradesman. Spring Reaches England. Triad. July. Or But A Wandering Voice. After the Shadow. A Moment in the Life of a Dog. Seeing the World. A Word for Fallen Grandeur. Where Do You Get the Clay? Decay in the Language. The Carving of the Ivory. The Prince of Stamboul. Lord Adrian.

58. *Selections from the Writings of Lord Dunsany*, edited by William Butler Yeats. Churchtown Dundrum (Ireland): The Cuala Press, 1912. Stories from previous collections.

59. *The Sword of Welleran and Other Tales of Enchantment*. New York: The Devin-Adair Company, 1954. Stories from previous collections.

60. *At The Edge of the World*, edited by Lin Carter. New York: Ballantine Books, 1970. Stories from previous collections.

61. *Beyond the Fields We Know*, edited by Lin Carter. New York: Ballantine Books, 1972. Stories from previous collections.

62. *Gods, Men, and Ghosts*, edited by E.F. Bleiler, Dover Books, 1972. Stories from previous collections.

63. *Over the Fields and Far Away*, edited by Lin Carter. Ballantine Books, 1974. Stories from previous collections.

64. *Verses Dedicatory*, edited by Lin Carter. Montclair NJ: Charnel House: Publishers, 1986. Short poems, originally written in Hazel Littlefield's copies of Dunsany's books.

PATHWAYS TO ELFLAND

Books about Lord Dunsany

1. Bierstadt, Edward. *Dunsany the Dramatist.* Boston: Little, Brown, and Company, 1917. Revised in 1919. Criticism.

2. Littlefield, Hazel. *Lord Dunsany: King of Dreams.* New York: Exposition Press, 1959. Memoir by a friend.

3. Amory, Mark. *Lord Dunsany: A Biography.* London: Collins, 1972.

Noteworthy Articles

1. de Camp, L. Sprague. "Two Men in One," in *Literary Swordsmen and Sorcerers.* Sauk City, WI: Arkham House, 1976.

2. Gogarty, Oliver St. John. "Lord Dunsany." *Atlantic Monthly,* March 1955.

Of Doubtful Provenance

1. Anonymous. *The Glittering Fake: A Fantasia by 'Fake.'* (Preface signed E.A.B.) Dublin: Talbot Press, 1918. Irish political satire using *The Glittering Gate* as a springboard. Occasionally attributed to Dunsany, but clearly not by him.

2. "Cable, Boyd." *Galleons.* Wrist-Watch Castaways, 1929. A persistent bibliographic ghost, often assumed to be a pseudonymous book-length poem, or a pamphlet of poetry. S.T. Joshi has identified it as follows: Cable, Boyd [a real author's name]. *Wrist-Watch Castaways* [title]. Oxford: Basil Blackwell, 1929. Dunsany's poem, "Galleons," is quoted, pp. 35-36.

Index

Note: In this index, titles of works are listed under the author's name, except in a few cases where the work and not the author is alluded to in the text. Such titles are listed alphabetically with the author's name in parentheses, as in "*All Quiet on the Western Front* (Remarque)," which is listed under "A."

Abbey Theatre, 40, 41, 42
Aethiopica (Heliodorus), 2
All Quiet on the Western Front (Remarque), 39
Amory, Mark, 60, 135
   Lord Dunsany: A Biography, 2, 21
The Arabian Nights, 2

Ba'hai religion, 107, 109
Beckett, Samuel, 73
Bellairs, John, 84
Benchley, Robert, 149
Benét, Stephen Vincent, 34
Ben Hur (stage play), 50-51
Beowulf, 14
Bible (King James version), 6, 8
Bierce, Ambrose, 15, 20
   "Moxon's Master," 123
Bierstadt, E. H., 52
   Dunsany the Dramatist, xii, 40, 59
Bleiler, E. F., 20, 28

The Blue Bird (Maeterlink), 148
Borges, Jorge Luis, 2
Buchwald, Art, 149
Burroughs, Edgar Rice, 112
Burton, Sir Richard F., x

Cabell, James Branch, 20, 109
Carter, Lin, 1, 2
   "The Gods of Niom Parma," 19
Collier, John, 34
Cooper, James Fenimore, 147

The Darling of the Gods (David Belasco and John Luther Long), 7
de Camp, Catherine C., viii, ix, xi
de Camp, L. Sprague, 16-17
   (with Willy Ley) *Lands Beyond*, vii
   (editor) *Warlocks and Warriors*, 19

PATHWAYS TO ELFLAND

de Mille, Cecil B., 50
The Demolished Man (Bester), 105
Dickens, Charles, 54
Don Quixote (Cervantes), 14, 77
Dunsany, Lady (Beatrice Villiers Plunkett), vii-xi, 3, 25
Dunsany, Lord (Edward John Moreton Drax Plunkett, 18th Baron) affected by World War I, 38-39
attitudes toward technology, 102-104
begins to write, 4
critical reputation, 1, (of his plays) 75
early life, 3-4
influences on, 6-7
involved in the Easter Rebellion, 38
Jorkens series of, 75, 87, 110-118, 155
political career, 3
radio scripts of, 71-72
science fiction of, vii, 104-105
Dunsany, Lord (Edward John Moreton Drax Plunkett, 18th Baron), works of:
"Advance Regulations," 151
Alexander, 53-56, 67, 75
Alexander and Three Small Plays, 69
The Amusements of Khan Karuda, 69, 101
"At the Time of the Full Moon," 128-129
Atmospherics, 72
"The Authorship of *Barrack Room Ballads*," 144
"Autumn Cricket," 124-125

"The Avenger of Perdóndaris," 34, 37
"The Battle of Killahoo," 150
"Bethmoora," 24
"Beyond the Fields We Know," 34, 37
"The Black Mamba," 112, 116
"Blagdaross," 25, 148
The Blessing of Pan, 85-86, 87, 88
The Book of Wonder, vii, 16, 19, 28, 29-32, 72, 146
"The Bride of the Man-Horse," 31
The Bureau de Change, 72
"The Bureau d'Echange de Maux," 72
"Carcassonne," 23
"The Carving of the Ivory," 42, 44
The Charwoman's Shadow, 83-85, 86, 155
Cheezo, 60-62
The Chronicles of Rodriguez (Don Rodriguez: The Chronicles of Shadow Valley), 76-78, 79, 83, 155
"Chu-Bu and Sheemish," 31
"The Cipher," 151
"The Coronation of Mr. Thomas Shap," 16, 31
"The Correct Kit," 113
"Correcting Nature," 124
"The Cricket Match," 147
The Curse of the Wise Woman, 85, 87-91, 105, 155, 157
"The Cut," 119
"The Day of the Poll," 27
"A Day on the Bog," 151

INDEX

"Decay in the Language," 144, 154
"The Distressing Tale of Thangobrind the Jeweller," 28-29
The Donnellan Lectures, 42, 142
A Dreamer's Tales, 22-28, 31, 34, 37, 105, 111, 133, 138
"The Eight Wishes," 147
The Evil Kettle, 69, 103
"Exchange No Robbery," 147
"The Exiles' Club," 33
"The Experiment," 121
"A Fable for Moderns," 125
"The Fall of Babbulkund," 13-14, 20, 24
Fame and the Poet, 62, 70
Fame Comes Late, 70
"The Fantastic Dreams," 98-99, 144, 152
Fifty-One Tales, 37, 120, 133, 147
Fifty Poems, 128-131
Five Plays, 56, 59
"The Fortress Unvanquishable, Save for Sacnoth," 13, 156
"Four Poets," 144, 145
The Fourth Book of Jorkens, 111, 117, 154
"The Ghost in the Old Corridor," 125
"The Ghosts," 22
The Ghosts of the Heaviside Layer and Other Fantasms, 63, 124-125, 144, 151, 154
The Ginger Cat, 56, 74
A Glimpse from the Watchtower, 144
The Glittering Gate, 41, 56
Gods, Men, and Ghosts, 155

"The Gods of Clay," 116
The Gods of Pegāna, 5, 7-10, 12, 22, 156
The Gods of the Mountain, 46-48, 49, 56
"The Golden City of Joy," 149
The Golden Doom, 48, 56
"The Gratitude of the Devil," 121
"Greek Meets Greek," 116-117
Guerrilla, 99-101, 156
"The Hashish Man," 25
"Helping the Fairies," 152-153
"The Highwayman," 21
His Fellow Men, 106-109
His Sainted Grandmother, 69
"The Hoard of the Gibbelins," 30-31
The Hopeless Passion of Mr. Bunion, 70
"The House of the Sphinx," 31
"How Ali Came to the Black Country," 102
"How Care Would Have Dealt with the Nomads," 147
"How Nuth Would Have Practised His Art upon the Gnoles," 19
"How One Came, As Was Foretold, to the City of Never," 31
"How Plash-Goo Came to the Land of None's Desire," 32
"How Ryan Got out of Russia," 115-116
"How the Office of Postman Fell Vacant at Otford-under-the-Wold," 34, 37
"Idle Days on the Yann," 24, 34

PATHWAYS TO ELFLAND

If, 64-66
If I Were Dictator, 142-143, 150
In Holy Russia, 72
"In Ravencore," 124
"In the Land of Time," 23
"In the Mojave," 125
"In Zaccarath," 23
"Into the Consommé," 150
"Jetsam," 148
Jorkens Borrows Another Whiskey, 111, 116
Jorkens Has a Large Whiskey, 111
"Jorkens' Problem," 125
Jorkens Remembers Africa, 111, 117-118
A Journey, 131
The Journey of the Soul, 72
King Argimenes and the Unknown Warrior, 42-43, 45-46, 51, 56
"The King of Sarahb," 113
The King of Elfland's Daughter, 78-83, 84, 86, 87, 155
"The Kith of the Elf-Folk," 21
The Last Book of Wonder, 32-34, 72, 102, 113, 120
The Last Revolution, xii, 102-106
"The Last Wolf," xii
The Laughter of the Gods, 49-51
"The Legend of the Dawn," 10
"A Let-Off," 150
Little Tales of Smethers, 121-124, 154, 155
"The Loot of Bombasharna," 32
Lord Adrian, 66-68, 69, 73
The Lost Silk Hat, 52-53, 56
"The Mad Ghost," 119
"The Man Who Ate the Phoenix," 118-119, 153
The Man Who Ate the Phoenix

(collection), 102, 118, 154, 155
A Matter of Honor, 70
Mr. Faithful, 68-69, 73, 74
"A Modern Portrait," 151
The Murderers, 48
My Ireland, 143-144
My Talks with Dean Spanley, 91, 95-96, 102, 119, 141, 155
"Near the Back of Beyond," 125
"The New Master," 103, 123, 124
A Night at the Inn, 51-52, 59
Nowadays, viii, ix, 134, 144
"Ode to a Dublin Critic," 130-131
The Old Folk of the Centuries, 62-63
The Old King's Tale, 59-60, 69
"The Old Man's Tale," 120
"On the Dry Land," 22
"The Opal Arrow Head," 120
"Our Distant Cousins," 113-114
"Our Laurels," 147
Patches of Sunlight, 3, 4, 6-7, 23, 103-104, 107, 130, 137-139
"The Pirate of the Round Pond," 124
Plays for Earth and Air, 69, 72
Plays of Gods and Men, 56
Plays of Near and Far, 61-62, 69
"Poltarnees, Beholder of Ocean," 22
"Poor Old Bill," 26-27
Power, 73
The Prince of Stamboul, 63-64
"Probable Adventure of the Three Literary Men," 30
The Pumpkin, 70-71

INDEX

The Queen's Enemies, 56, 59
"The Rations of Murdoch Fin-ucan," 151
"The Return," 119, 125
"The Revenge," 151
"The Road," 39, 143
The Road (play), 72
"Romance," 148
Rory and Bran, 91-93, 97
"A Royal Swan," 151
"The Sack of Emeralds," 34
Selections from the Writings of Lord Dunsany, 24
Seven Modern Comedies, 69
The Seventh Symphony, 71
"The Shield of Athene," 124
"The Shop in Go-by Street," 34
The Sirens Wake, 3, 128, 137, 141-142
"The Slugly Beast," 115
"Snow White up to Date," 119-120, 121
"Songs from an Evil Wood," 129-130
"The Sorrow of the Search," 16, 23
The Story of Mona Sheehy, 96-97, 118
"The Story of Tse Gah," 152
The Strange Journeys of Colonel Polders, 101-102
The Strange Lover, 72
"The Sword of Welleran," 43
The Sword of Welleran (collection), 12-14, 17, 18, 21, 22, 31, 37
"A Tale of Land and Sea," 32-33
"The Tale of the Abu Laheeb," 112
Tales of Three Hemispheres, 34-37, 110, 121, 148, 149
Tales of War, 38, 43
Tales of Wonder, see *The Last Book of Wonder*
The Tents of the Arabs, 48-49, 59
"Thirteen at Table," 33
"The Three Infernal Jokes," 33
"Three Men in a Garden," 125
"The Three Sailors' Gambit," 33, 34
"The Three Sisters," 132
Time and the Gods, 10-12, 15, 16, 17, 21, 23
To Awaken Pegasus, 131, 133
The Travel Tales of Mr. Joseph Jorkens, 111
"Told Under Oath," 124
"Two Bottles of Relish," 122-123
"Two Sketches," 149
"Ulysses, Bound to the Mast," 132
Unhappy Far-Off Things, 38
Up in the Hills, 91, 93-95, 100, 107, 138, 143
The Use of Man, 71
"The Warning," 115
"What Jorkens Has to Put up with," 112-113
"Where the Tides Ebb and Flow" ("The Terrible Dream"), 25-26, 134-135, 147
While the Sirens Slept, 3, 75, 111-112, 137, 139-141
"Why the Milkman Shudders When He Perceives the Dawn," 32

PATHWAYS TO ELFLAND

"The Widow Flynn's Apple Tree," 102, 119

"The Wind in the Wood," 119

"The Wonderful Window," 31, 72

"A Word for Fallen Grandeur," 144

The Year, 131

Dunsany, Lord (Randal Plunkett, 19th Baron), x, 140

Eliot, T. S., 125, 135-136

Elkin Matthews, 8

Ellery Queen's Mystery Magazine, 125

The Epic of Gilgamesh, 14

France, Anatole, 29

Gesar of Ling (Tibetan epic), 14

The Golden Ass (Apuleius), 2

Good Housekeeping, 152

The Great Dictator (film), 150

Gregory, Lady Augusta, 40, 46

Grimm brothers, 6

Harper's Bazaar, 63

Harper's Magazine, 121

Herodotus, 6, 56

Howard, Robert E., 15

Ibsen, Henrik, 45

Hedda Gabler, 44

Iliad (Homer), 14

Index, 173

Ionesco, Eugene, 73

The Irish Review, 34, 42

John O'London's Weekly, 152

Joshi, S. T., 146

Kafka, Franz, 26

Kipling, Rudyard, 144

Kirk, Tim, 37

Ledwidge, Francis, 143

Le Guin, Ursula K., 18, 20

"From Elfland to Poughkeepsie," 17

Leiber, Fritz, 15

Lewis, C. S., 104

"Lord Dunsany" (Oliver St. John Gogarty), xii, 145

Lord Dunsany: King of Dreams (Hazel Littlefield), 73, 133

The Lord of the Rings (Tolkien), 74

Lovecraft, H. P., 9, 15-17, 29, 32, 34-37, 111, 139

"Celephais," 16

The Commonplace Book, 34

"The Dream Quest of Unknown Kadath," 16

"The Other Gods," 16

"The Man Who Sold Rope to the Gnoles" (Margaret St. Clair, writing as "Idris Seabright"), 19

"Medusa" (Walter Roberts), 124

Metamorphoses (Ovid), 10

The Moonstone (Collins), 51

The New York Times, 64, 68

Nourse, Alan E., x

Oates, Titus, xi

Odyssey (Homer), 14

O'Neill, Eugene, 73

[178]

INDEX

Orlando Furioso, (Ariosto), 14

The Pall Mall Magazine, 4
Plunkett, Edward John Moreton
Drax, *see Dunsany*
Plunkett, (Saint)Oliver, xi
Plunkett, Randal, *see Dunsany*
Poe, Edgar Allan, 15
Pratt, Fletcher, 117
    (with de Camp) *Tales from Gav-agan's Bar*, 117
    The Well of the Unicorn, 46
Punch, 149, 150, 152, 153
The Puppet Masters (Heinlein), 105

The Red Badge of Courage (Crane), 147-148
Romantics, 20, 29
Russell, George (AE), 143, 144

Saturday Review, 146, 147, 148, 152
Shakespeare, William, 45
    Macbeth, 45
    The Tempest, 105
Shaw, George Bernard, 3, 45, 74, 145
Sheridan, Richard Brinsley, 45
Short Plays for Junior and Senior High Schools (Webber and Webster), 63
Sime, Sidney, xi, 21, 28, 37
Smith, Clark Ashton, xi, 15, 17
Sophocles, 44
The Spectator, 152

Stephens, James, 29, 144
Stewart, George, 104
    The Earth Abides, 104
The Strand, 152
Swinburne, Algernon C., 11
sword and sorcery, 15
Synge, John Millington, 41, 148
    Deirdre of the Sorrows, 148

Tales from the White Hart (Clarke), 117
Thurber, James, 149
Time and Tide, 152
Tomorrow, 152
Twain, Mark, 2
    A Connecticut Yankee in King Arthur's Court, 2
    The Mysterious Stranger, 2

Vanity Fair, 148
Vergil, 148
Voltaire, 2

Weirdbook, 124
Wells, H. G., 64
White, T. H., 84
Wilde, Oscar, 7, 29, 64, 74
    The Importance of Being Earnest, 52
    The Witch of Ramoth (Van Doren), 34

Yeats, William Butler, 7, 24, 40-41, 46, 145

FIN

[180]